For the Admiral

'Indispensable…Drawing on her extensive experience of working in immigration detention, Stephanie Lam will help you identify your own key stressors and suggest simple, practical ways to lessen the pressure so you can become clearer-thinking, more relaxed and enjoy life once more.'

Sarah Rayner, author of Making Friends with Anxiety.

'Recommended for anyone feeling overwhelmed by the world: practical, calming, with a wonderful writing style.'

Kate Harrison, author of the 5:2 series.

'A fascinating, moving, much-needed book.'

Siobhan Curham, author of Something More.

Stephanie Lam is a wellbeing and creativity journalist. She writes the popular *Everyday Escape* back-page column for *Breathe* magazine on real-world ways to achieve headspace and happiness, and for twenty years has also worked as a teacher alongside highly-stressed people held in immigration detention.

She wasn't always so calm. In 2015, after her debut novel *The Mysterious Affair At Castaway House* was published by Penguin Books, and with no time for anything to go wrong, a crisis transformed her life and forced her to rethink everything she thought she knew. From being a super-frazzled perfectionist who thought being busy was her special skill, she then became an expert on stress and how to escape it. She went on to devise *Unfrazzle*, an easy six-step plan to help everyone, no matter what their frazzle status, reclaim true calm within everyday life.

Find out more about Stephanie on her website *stephanielam-author.com* or search the web using the hashtag *#Unfrazzle*.

Liz

Thanks for coming to the workshop!

Best wishes,

Stephanie Lam

UNFRAZZLE

The easy way to reclaim your calm

STEPHANIE LAM

ISBN 978-1-9163194-0-0 (paperback)

ISBN 978-1-9163194-1-7 (ebook)

Published by Rivers & Stone Books

www.riversandstone.space

Contents

INTRODUCTION

WELCOME TO UNFRAZZLE

Do you feel a long way from your true self? Do you want to properly appreciate the good moments, and cope better with the bad? Do you ever feel overwhelmed, that your brain is too full, or that life isn't right and you don't know why? Are you too strung-out to even think about change, but you know that something has to give?

I was like that once.

As I write these words, I'm looking at a photograph of me in 2015. In the photo, I'm on my way to an event at the Brighton Festival, where I'm about to do a reading from my debut novel. In many respects, I have the life I once dreamt of – to have a novel published, plus a rewarding second job working with men held in immigration detention.

Yet the person in that photograph was out of balance in her own life. She was always tired and in thrall to her phone. She was excited, but not calm. She felt she was running to catch up, but never quite made it.

Not long after that Brighton Festival event, a crisis transformed my life. It unravelled the little calm I had left, and day by day, month by month, ramped up my stress levels until there was only one place left to go: down.

Yet all that happened – as little as I wanted it – became a huge learning experience. It happened precisely because I was plucked from the familiar path I thought I was travelling, and thrown into the wilderness: a desert landscape with no signposts to show the way. I had to carve my own route out, helped by my work in immigration detention, which showed me the process by which people cope – and even thrive – amid acute, mind-bending stress.

I rediscovered the route to true calm, even when surrounded by everyday stress. I found the steps to creating a nurturing space within – not as an extra to – existing routines. And I started becoming the me I always wanted to be: that is, in balance. It's been a long journey, and it's one I'll keep travelling for the rest of my life.

While in that wilderness, I read and researched and tried every method I could to help me come down from stress and keep me on track. What I needed, however, was a book that gave an overall view of frazzle, one that I felt understood what it was like to live in the real world, connecting up the areas I thought were the most important: sleep, smartphones, head space, and reconnecting to that calmer self I knew was inside. *Unfrazzle* is the book I wish I'd had at the beginning, the one that would have shown me the way.

I wrote *Unfrazzle* to share with you what I've learned. I believe it will help you too to reclaim your life and discover inner harmony, no matter the chaos outside.

In a nutshell:
Change is possible, whatever your state of frazzle. The Unfrazzle method is a real-world plan that will enable you to rediscover the calmer self you have inside.

What will this book do for you?

It WILL:

Give you plenty of quizzes and activities to assess your state of frazzle, plus easy-to-understand exercises and routines to get you into a calmer state.

You can read this book in any order, but it will make more sense if you read it through at least once from start to finish – and then, if you want to truly rewire your brain for calm and harmony, travel layer by layer through the book: from the basics of Unfrazzle, to a plan for thriving throughout the rest of your life.

It WON'T:

Ask you to add yet another thing to your to-do list. Instead, it will teach you how to adapt your already-existing routines (including the ones you don't currently enjoy) to provide you with a nurturing space to recharge and unwind.

You'll also discover how to:
Cope in a crisis
Get control of your phone
Sort your sleep
Take time out every day of your life
...And reconnect with your whole self

You'll learn super-easy chunks about the neuroscience of stress, read true-life tales of frazzle (including my own journey to Unfrazzle), and learn a little of what life is like in the high-stress state of being detained in an immigration removal centre.

You'll also get dozens of tips to easily manage and reduce everyday barriers to calm and balance.

One thing you can do before you start

Buy a pen and a special notebook. There'll be exercises where you'll need to write down your answers, but in addition I suggest using it to record your feedback on the ideas and new routines. You can jot down any extra notes, and write up anything that interests you or you want to remember.

Why should you listen to me?

I'm not a medical professional or a psychologist. I haven't made a fortune out of selling my *'One Magic Solution!'* to desperate people. I'm a normal person, with a normal life. I live in the real world: mundane, gritty, less than ideal, and with a dozen demands on my time.

But I've been into the pit of stress, and I've come out the other side an expert in the biochemistry and neuroscience of frazzle. I also have two decades' worth of experience working with people at the extreme end of stress. I've discovered how we've wired our brain for maximum frazzle, and I've learned the two basic principles of Unfrazzle – which you'll read about in Chapter One.

Through desperation, I ended up devising dozens of emergency remedies, and I've found that they work on anyone who's at the extreme end of frazzle. I'm also lucky enough to write a column for *Breathe* magazine where I share a version of these, which I call *Everyday Escapes* – basically, methods I've learned for reclaiming calm and inner harmony by embracing the less-than-ideal aspects of life, rather than wishing for an alternative reality to make everything right.

All the above, plus the desire I had for a book that could have helped me when I was really struggling, meant I've also developed a coherent plan, which you'll find in these pages. This book encompasses all aspects of unfrazzling, from first-base balance to a deeper, brain-changing sense of peace. Because I know how hard it is to carve out extra time when we don't have any, I've located each part of the plan within everyday habits and routines. In addition, you can follow the plan as minimally or as maximally as you want. You can try one chapter, one activity, one quiz – or read the entire book from start to finish, as it builds from the basics to the real deep stuff of Unfrazzle.

But I guess that the main thing I've learned is that coming into a calmer state is essential for all of us. I used to have the idea that some of these routines and fixes seemed indulgent, perhaps even decadent, because they make you take time and space away from work, phones and busyness, even when it seems impossible. Now I know they're not. Unfrazzling is essential to clearing the detritus in our brain and rewiring us for balance and inner peace.

How to survive extreme stress: lessons from immigration detention

Twenty years ago I started working in an Immigration Removal Centre – or immigration detention, as it is often known. These are centres of detention for foreign nationals. People often ask me *Who do you have there? Refugees? Visa overstayers?* The truth is, I've met every type of person you can imagine.

People also often assume that these centres are pits of horror where people languish in dank cells. In truth, there are strict Detention Centre rules which lay down requirements for the care and wellbeing of residents. These include access to an extensive programme of activities and education, of which I am a part. Certainly, in the centre where I work the staff are highly trained in focusing on support for the residents, and I've witnessed many of my colleagues show immense kindness in the course of their duties. Plenty of them go out of their way to help the people in their care.

On the other hand, *Detention in jail or other institution* ranks joint fourth – along with death of a close family member – on the famous 1967 Holmes & Rahe Social Readjustment Rating Scale, often known as the Life Stress Inventory.[1] In addition, Immigration Removal Centres do not have a fixed term of imprisonment. Many people who arrive have little idea of how long they will remain inside, and are uncertain as to their future.

Uncertainty about one's future situation causes an exponentially larger amount of stress than certainty – even if the certainty is unpleasant, as a 2016 study by University College London showed.[2] In addition, over the past two decades I've been told almost every day by different residents of how stressed they feel over being detained. I've also witnessed the effects that the stress of uncertainty can have.

However, I've also been inspired, uplifted and educated. A minority of the residents are able to cope with and manage their stress better than others. That's partly due to personal

1   https://www.stress.org/holmes-rahe-stress-inventory
2   https://www.ucl.ac.uk/news/2016/mar/uncertainty-can-cause-more-stress-inev-itable-pain

circumstances, but mostly because they understand what to do to manage an extremely difficult situation.

What I've learned from them about coping with a highly stressful situation underpins this book.

In the list below are ideas for coping if you're undergoing extreme stress on a long-term, ongoing basis; tips I've picked up over my years of working in immigration detention. They won't solve your problem, but they may help you to cope better with the situation.

How to cope with extreme stress
- Take on regular, non-harmful routines
- Keep focused on achievable goals
- Find a space for quiet contemplation, meditation or prayer
- Stay physically fit and active
- Occupy the brain in a simple way
- Keep open-minded to new experiences

I've also learned specific tips and techniques from the men, some of which I include in the book. As Adam, one of the residents said to me a while ago: *Whatever helps people in detention to get by will help everyone.*

A note on the 'detention stories' in this book.

Due to my job, I am not allowed – and nor would I want – to share any personal information about any of the residents I've met there. Yet much of what I have learned from the guys has informed the basis of this book, and I believe that their direct stories will help you to understand the mechanics of acute stress, and how to cope with it.

The personal stories you'll read throughout this book from people in detention are therefore composite tales, gleaned from the thousands of people I've met over my twenty years working there. Although each person is unique, with wildly varying backgrounds, their experiences of detention are remarkably similar, and the way they interpret that experience often follows a similar trajectory. It follows that if any of us were in that sort of situation, we would respond in one of only a number of ways. Nobody is immune from the effects of stress, but everyone can take steps to help them cope with it.

Therefore, everything you'll read is true, but I have taken elements from many people's real-life stories, and distilled them into just a few. I have written them this way to help the message of each story come across with more clarity, and to place you somewhere I hope you'll never have to be.

CHAPTER ONE

THE BASICS OF FRAZZLE: HOW TO BEGIN

i) What's your frazzle status?

Before addressing any problem, let's first ascertain how deep it goes. Do the quiz below to work out your frazzle status.

Quiz: Get your frazzle status

Look at the symptoms of frazzle below. Rate each symptom for yourself on a scale from 0 – 4.

4 = strongly agree   3 = agree   2 = neither agree nor disagree   1 = disagree   0 = strongly disagree

1. I feel more easily irritated than I used to.
2. I feel there are too many demands on my time.
3. I crave peace and solitude.
4. I feel life is too fast for me.
5. I get 'racing thoughts'.
6. I find it hard to sleep restfully at night.
7. Using social media sometimes makes me feel uncomfortable or unhappy.
8. I sometimes feel nervous before I open my inbox.
9. I often get anxious.
10. I get easily fatigued.
11. I sometimes feel overwhelmed with life.
12. I worry about things more than I used to.
13. My brain sometimes feels 'full up'.
14. I am easily stressed out.
15. I would feel lost without my phone.
16. I find it hard to make simple decisions.
17. I feel there are too many problems I can't solve.

Add up your points and get your frazzle status below:

0-17: LOW FRAZZLE You're able to navigate a highly-stimulating world without it impinging on your sense of calm. The exercises and routines in this book will help you to continue as you are, while recognising if stress and frazzle ever start to creep in.

18-34: SOME FRAZZLE You have access to a healthy element of Unfrazzle, but when stress heightens, you certainly feel its effects. This book will give you the perfect opportunity to make the most of the clarity you have, and eliminate the frazzle that remains in order to recover the calm and balance that's well within reach.

35-49: MEDIUM FRAZZLE Frazzle has sneaked into your life, but it can sneak out again too. This book is your chance to get back to the person you were until a short time ago, and to manage any challenges that may come your way.

50-59: HIGH FRAZZLE You yearn for a clearer, calmer brain, but there's never enough time to think about how you'd do that. This book will take the 'thinking' element away, by altering your daily routines towards Unfrazzle.

60-68: EXTREME FRAZZLE Frazzle is a way of life for you. You're clinging on by your fingernails, and you're desperate for help. You're the reason I wrote this book. I was so frazzled I couldn't think straight – and when I did manage to unfrazzle I wanted to help others by sharing all I'd learned. If I can turn it around by following this plan, so can you. If you need emergency action, however, turn to page 30 and read *In case of emergency: how to survive extreme frazzle.*

ii) When frazzle goes too far

Looking at your answers to the quiz might be enough for you to want to turn the clock back on your frazzle. Good news: this is perfectly possible. You can rewire your brain to seek Unfrazzle, to swerve round frazzle even before you see it coming, and to embed nurturing routines into your life until they seem second nature. How? The answer lies in your miraculous plastic brain.

How to rewire a brain

Over the course of your life, your brain creates habits and routines. It sparks reactions that seem automatic because they're so deeply entrenched. They can, in fact, seem hard-wired – but quite the opposite is true.

Until fairly recently, most neurologists assumed that as we aged, neurons and synapses did not develop. Instead, they died off as we got older and our brain began to degenerate. 'Miracle' stories of paralysis recovery were seen as just that: miracles.

However, it has now been established that although your neurons continue to die from the moment you're born, the neurons that remain can develop more and more branches, reaching out to other neurons across our brain map. If one part of the brain dies (as with paralysis), another part of the brain can take over those lost functions. In science, this is called neuroplasticity; basically, it means that the brain always has potential for change.

Therefore, it might seem obvious, but all the same it's important to remember this: You weren't born frazzled.

Frazzle is a state that any brain can learn to be in, reinforced by repetition, routine and association. Neuronal frazzling connections become stronger the more we practise, and eventually the brain achieves what is known as long-term potentiation – or what might seem an automatic behaviour or reaction.

Whatever stage of frazzle you're at, your brain has learned to be that way. However, it can also unlearn it. Your brain has equally huge potential to be calm, relaxed and in a state of Unfrazzle. You get there by the same route you got in: repetition, routine and association – along with a firm basis for good brain health, which means exercise, the right fuel and space to feel truly calm.

You'll learn more about this as you travel through the book. For now, keep the following in mind: If you have an unhelpful habit, or a way of thinking, or any other neural connection that you want to stop, you can do so if you allow that area of the brain map to fall into disuse. If new connections are never formed, the branches wither and die. Eventually, the habit falls away.

The theory here is sound: it's doing it that's the tricky thing. And this is the reason I wrote this book – to help rewire a frazzled brain.

How stress affects the brain

But what happens if you don't address your frazzle? If you're always frazzled, the brain and body operate in a state of chronic stress. You might have heard of the autonomic nervous system which runs the body. It is divided into two parts. The **sympathetic** system, which works from the upper third of the brain stem, activates the 'fight-or-flight', stress-hormone response. The **parasympathetic** system, which operates from the lower two-thirds of the brain stem, activates the 'rest-and-digest', calm response.

The two systems cannot work at the same time: one inhibits the other. Put simply, your brain is either stressed or relaxed. In a state of Unfrazzle, 90% of activity runs via the parasympathetic system. But if your frazzle status is at medium or above, your brain is operating with its stress switched to 'on'. Then, as the stress neurotransmitters adrenaline and noradrenaline continue to activate their receiving neurons, your brain becomes stressed more easily, with less and less input.

Basically, as time goes on, and the longer you live with chronic stress, **the more frazzled you start to feel.**

Perhaps you've recognised this in yourself. If your frazzle peaks at aspects of life that didn't use to bother you so much – the daily commute, the supermarket shop, crowds, noise, the news – you might be thinking it's because life is more difficult.

In some ways, that might be true. But what's really changed is the brain: it's switched the stress response permanently ON, and the brain requires less and less stimulus to activate those symptoms of frazzle.

Dr Datis Kharrazian, an expert on brain health, explains that this is because the brain's limbic system – otherwise known as our survival centre – develops 'negative plasticity' for stress. '[It] becomes increasingly efficient at responding to stress,' he writes in *Why Isn't My Brain Working?*, his book on the reasons for brain decline and how to reverse it. 'It takes less stress over time to create the same response,' he adds. 'Obviously, this is not a good thing as it means you'll get stressed out more easily over smaller stuff. Eventually it becomes permanently active and easily generates a stress response with very little stimulus.'

Worryingly, he also adds, 'When this vicious cycle of stress overcomes the brain, brain inflammation is the outcome.'

How stress affects the body

If you become used to living with stress you won't recognise it for what it is. It feels normal, but it isn't. Living with stress means constant activation of the stress hormones, which in turn means that levels of cortisol become significantly elevated in the body. Elevated levels of stress hormones can lead you to feeling hyper or anxious, moody or depressed. Cortisol affects the sleep-wake cycle, so too much means the brain will stop you either falling asleep or staying asleep, and can make you feel as if your brain is more alive after 9 or 10pm.

Other hormones can also be affected – including testosterone, oestrogen and progesterone. An imbalance of these can cause a variety of symptoms, including a feeling that your brain is 'full up' or foggy.

If the problem continues, the body's struggle with stress can lead eventually to chronic exhaustion, memory problems, weight gain, gut disturbances, inflammation, and migraines.

Functional medicine practitioner Robyn Puglia, who has treated hundreds of patients with chronic, long-term illnesses, says:

> *There are four primary non-genetic issues which will cause someone to get sick: the wrong food, toxins, infection, and stress. Overexposure to just one of these can make you long term, chronically ill.*

Chronic stress can even cause the non-genetic form of Alzheimer's Disease. Professor of Neurology Dale Bredesen, an expert on the mechanisms of Alzheimer's, says that chronic stress is an important contributor to cognitive decline.

'Stress increases levels of cortisol, which at high levels is toxic to our brains – in particular the memory-consolidating hippocampus, which is one of the first structures to be assaulted by Alzheimer's Disease,' he writes in his book *The End of Alzheimer's*. 'Stress also increases a number of risk factors for cognitive decline and Alzheimer's disease.'

These include increasing blood glucose levels, body fat, risk of obesity, carbohydrate craving and more. He adds that toxic levels of stress also attack the factors that preserve our brain, and thereby prevent the ravaging effects of the disease.

This might sound melodramatic, and it doesn't mean that if you're at high frazzle you'll end up with a long-term illness. But being stressed will make you more vulnerable to many health problems, from minor to major. Stress drastically lowers the immune system – perhaps you've already noticed that when you get a cold you find it harder to shake off than you used to. As your poor immune system battles one virus, it's more vulnerable to attack on another front.

If the crisis I lived through hadn't happened, I am 100% certain that I would still be unknowingly living with my own frazzle creep, and all its attendant symptoms: fatigue, overwhelm, anxiety, irritation, sleeplessness and viruses I couldn't shake off.

There's more. Although through my work in immigration detention I've seen how toxic levels of stress affect people's day-to-day existence, I still truly had no idea what it's like to go through a life-changing crisis, with no fixed end date.

After that happened to me, my understanding of the stress of detention took another leap. I still have no idea of what it's really like to be in that situation, but I do know how it feels to have the rug pulled from under your feet.

How (not) to survive a crisis: my story

2015 was supposed to be a good year for me. I turned 40, and threw a party for my friends and family in a Moroccan bar. My novel had been published the year before, and people seemed to like it. I was writing another, plus speaking at literary events and attending friends' book launches. I was teaching in an incredibly fulfilling role, and in my spare time I was doing PR and campaigning work for a charity.

Quite frankly, I didn't have time for anything to go wrong.

Then overnight my partner became seriously ill, and was rushed to Accident & Emergency. We were then passed on from department to department to department, but each doctor we saw, albeit sympathetic, was unable to help us with either a diagnosis or a solution.

We went home with a prescription for painkillers that didn't work, and I tried to carry on with my life. I thought that to stop doing things would be to 'give in' somehow – although who or what I'd be giving in to, I had no idea. Here was just another (massive) factor to add in to my busy schedule. But I was good at being busy! It was like a magic skill! And here I was, showing the world that I could manage even when the load became really, *really* heavy.

We both operated, in effect, in crisis mode for over two years. It was the uncertainty that ramped up our levels of stress: we found a few answers but no real solutions, no end date, and no idea of when this would be over.

The cracks in my wellbeing started to show immediately, but I refused to notice them. Managing the crisis meant nothing got done at home but the bare minimum. For months a suitcase stood in the middle of the living room because after going on a writing retreat I hadn't had the brain space to unpack the few clothes inside.

I adjusted, in a manner of speaking. I stopped the voluntary work. I started getting up at five o'clock in the morning to write before I went to work. I was high as a kite and wired to my eyeballs with stress, but I was coping. Because coping was what I did.

I started getting furious for no reason. A friend texted with sympathy but hadn't used quite the 'right' tone. I went off the scale with rage (luckily I didn't tell her). A broken teacup became a tragedy of epic proportions. You name it, I felt it. Frazzle status? Around 67, I'd say – except I didn't say, because I didn't know I needed to.

Nine months into the chaos, after much persuasion from my partner, I went to my GP and was signed off sick from work with stress. And that, as dreadful as it was, became the first turning point in my story of Unfrazzle.

iii) In case of emergency: how to survive extreme frazzle

Return to the quiz you answered a few pages ago. Are you at *very high* or *extreme* frazzle? If so, here's what I learned during my own crisis on how to survive a precarious situation. The following is not about Unfrazzle; it's about putting the brakes on a runaway train. Open in case of emergency.

1. Write down all and any triggers that raise you from *high* to *extreme* frazzle.
2. Remove or reduce as many as you can **right now**. Remember – this is an emergency solution. It's not a long-term plan.
3. Remember also that **you are not indispensable**.

In addition...

4. Ask for help (I've learned that pride gets you nowhere). You might try:
- your GP.
- your workplace – some offer counselling services.
- the Samaritans if you're in the UK or Ireland – however minor you feel your problems to be. (Call **116 123** for free at any time of day or night).
- places of worship can offer a safe space and someone to talk to if you have faith, or even if you don't.
- your partner, friends or family may help to remove some of the practical pressures you're under.

The extreme frazzle quick-fix spa retreat

During that summer of stress, while off from work, I came back to myself a bit. Weirdly, though, I still didn't take my frazzle status seriously, perhaps because that would have meant accepting how desperate the situation was, and also because it was hard enough trying to find help for my partner, let alone anything I felt was of lesser importance.

However, I did work out a fundamental truth during that time. Up to that point we'd been living in the domestic equivalent of a war room: lots of strategising and crisis management, but not much time out. While off work, with more brain space, I realised that what might help would be a calm, quiet environment in order to heal.

Hardly the revelation of the century. Yet to this end, I abruptly stopped all my researching and pep talks, and instead created a nurturing, healing space at home. For months, our city-centre flat became as mindful, still and quiet as it's possible for a city-centre flat to be. We lived like Zen monks, sort of, and I renamed our flat the **Spa Retreat**, because, deep down, I really wanted to be on a proper retreat, perhaps in the Swiss Alps surrounded by pine trees, where someone else would take care of everything. Failing that, I created a retreat in our second-floor flat overlooking the constant rush of traffic on the main road.

It helped my partner. But much more than that: it worked for me.

Bit by bit, my frazzle status receded – ever so slightly, but it was enough for me to realise that a spa retreat wasn't only for other people. In fact, anyone who is veering towards extreme frazzle should write the following rules out and stick them on the fridge.

Do it. Even for a day, just do it. It won't solve the underlying problem, but it will give your head some necessary space.

Do you need a quick fix for extreme frazzle?
If you can, take a day, a few days or a week off and go somewhere (even your own home) to be alone. Follow the rules below.

Rules of the Retreat:
- eat nourishing meals that you love.
- admit no visitors (virtual or in the flesh).
- speak and move slowly – have you noticed how people never rush around while on retreat?
- only do healing activities: colouring in, reading, favourite funny films.
- no social media (See Chapter Two for help on this).
- ensure a regular bedtime (Chapter Three will show you why and how to achieve this).
- have long, slow baths (see Chapter Four for how using Epsom salts can also help).
- do daily breath meditations (see Chapter Five for one you can try).

iv) The two principles to a life of Unfrazzle

After the spa retreat, and as I picked myself up and returned to work, I went on an exploration of traditional (and not-so-traditional) ways to calm down from stress. I also read up on neuroplasticity, and how routines and repetition wire behaviours – for good or ill – into the brain.

My instincts told me that things had to change. The challenges weren't over: we had some answers, and some help, but things were still very bad. I needed to learn to cope with crisis on a long-term basis, and if I didn't learn techniques to rebalance my life I'd end up in the same position I'd been in before.

As I researched neuroscience and nutrition, sleep theory and smartphone addiction, as I tried mindfulness, shiatsu, talking therapies and pretty much anything I could, I became convinced of the need to come down from stress in every area of my life.

I went for it. Everything I could do, I did, and I aimed to do it all properly – perfectly. I'd be the best calm person ever! And then I'd be able to handle anything – even an ongoing crisis like this one, plus teaching, plus writing. And when the crisis was over, life would be new and amazing. Perhaps I'd end up living in a rose-twined cottage, Instagramming my glutenfree/sugarfree/vegan banana bread to the world, hashtagged *#lovemylife*.

A few months later, with my periods stopped from being so underweight with stress, I was signed off sick from work once more.

Like prising my hands from a boulder, I slowly, reluctantly came to the realisation that I hadn't really changed. I was still super busy with extraordinarily high standards, only now they were focused in another direction.

It was a wake-up call, and I knew change had to come from within.

I stopped writing for months, because writing, rather than a pleasure, had become just another hard-work chore. I came off all social media for a while. I reflected on what *really* calmed my central nervous system, instead of what I wanted to work. And slowly, I decided to try to build my life around two core principles of Unfrazzle:

Embrace imperfection

Do less stuff

My entire life since childhood had been based on the principle: *'If it's not perfect, it's not worth it.'* As I grew to adulthood and accumulated responsibilities and roles, I also became ever more drawn to the high of adrenaline that I got when I was rushing around, and so I added another principle: *'Busy is good.'*

'If it's not perfect, it's not worth it.'

This is when you:

- try and make the perfect decision, in a world overflowing with choice
- give yourself or others a hard time for not matching up to your standards
- think there is a 'right' way, and you just have to find it

Why perfectionism frazzles

Perfectionism is constant work for your poor old brain. Specifically, for your so-called clever brain that has to prioritise, sort, make decisions, get it 'right', and the emotional brain that sends you stress signals when you get it 'wrong.'

Dropping the neural connections that lead towards perfectionism will lead you to a calmer life. Relax your perfectionist tendencies, and you will start to find the route to Unfrazzle.

'Busy is good.'

This is when you:

- think 'doing nothing' means you have time to catch up on your emails
- don't leave enough time for an activity
- love your ability to multi-task, as if it's a special skill (more on this in Chapter Five)

Why 'busy is good' frazzles

Lots of people are busy. Parents of young children. Workers. Working parents. It can seem as if the entire planet is on a treadmill of busy – and not one, by the way, that appears to be leading us anywhere good.

But how much of that busy is inevitable, and how much is us convincing ourselves it's inevitable? It's a difficult area to tease apart, and one that plenty of the exercises in this book aim to do. But here is the reason why the principle *busy is good* will frazzle you:

The brain isn't supposed to be kept constantly at work – whether that's checking emails, multi-tasking or rushing around. The prefrontal cortex needs downtime – and not only at night. It needs to be kept rested so that it can do all its chores properly. Keep any motor running and it will wear out. Not only that, but busyness overwhelms the emotional brain too: rushing, never leaving enough time – these cause an influx of stress hormones including adrenaline and cortisol. Adren-aline is addictive, and a body running on stress hormones will become frazzled. After not so long, the brain becomes fatigued and feels 'full up'. Under-stimulation allows your brain to recharge.

Take time to recharge by doing less, and you will unfrazzle.

Quiz – What are your CURRENT frazzle values?

One of the exciting things about neuroplasticity is that *everything can change, including your 'frazzle values'. Do the quiz to discover what your current ones are.*

Look at the following pairs of values. Think about where you are on the spectrum for each statement – towards the left, the right, or somewhere in the middle?

Look at the example answers for the first three pairs of statements. The respondent **usually** thinks they must live life to the full, is **occasionally** not bothered about being bored, and **always** aims to do their best.

Example answers:

I must live life to the full	I am not bothered at all
X	
I hate being bored	I don't care if I'm bored
	X
I aim to always do my best	I often think 'that'll do'
X	

Your answers:

I must live life to the full	I am not bothered at all
I hate being bored	I don't care if I'm bored
I aim to always do my best	I often think 'that'll do'
I don't want to make a mistake	I rarely notice any mistakes
I research all my options thoroughly	I choose the first thing I see
I have bucket lists	I have very few ambitions
I hate missing out	I don't care if I miss out
I change my mind frequently	I stick to my first decision
I like to keep busy	I am rarely busy
I want to maximise my time	I never think about this
I hate waiting for people	I am happy to wait for people
I hate being early	I don't mind being early
I have high standards	I have low standards

The statements on the left are 'frazzle values'. In your notebook, write all that apply to you.

I am not suggesting that the values on the right are those to aim for. I like having high standards *for certain things*. I like to research my options a bit, sometimes. It's when those values are applied across the board, to an extreme, that you'll be living through frazzle. Shifting yourself towards the Unfrazzle values – at least in some areas of your life – will enable you to follow the two basic principles to a life of Unfrazzle:

Embrace imperfection

Do less stuff

These principles underpin the book. Each layer of Unfrazzle will guide you deeper into a recharging for your brain, and give your brain space to work properly. It's by following these two principles that I've realised how much they can lead us to a truer, more balanced self.

v) Get your Unfrazzle balance

What do you already do to unfrazzle? Exercise is key – perhaps swimming, a yoga class, running, or walking in nature. Maybe you meditate or pray. Do you have a calming hobby, such as gardening or colouring in?

Before my crisis hit, I swam regularly and went to yoga once a week. I came out of an exercise session invigorated, with a clear brain. It was an essential part of my routine (it still is) – but at the same time, I was totally frazzled.

Why? Because my life was out of balance. The vast majority of my other routines were geared towards frazzle: when I did household chores; when I commuted; when I rushed out of the house because I was late; when I said yes to everything; when I behaved like a perfectionist; when I was constantly occupied; when I used my phone; when I scrambled to fit it all in.

My exercise routine was never going to be enough to tip me towards Unfrazzle, because the balance was tipped the other way. It's basic mathematics: the more your routines are designed for Unfrazzle, the more unfrazzled you'll be. Exercise is an 'extra'. If it's something you squeeze into our life, it means your Unfrazzle will be an extra too.

It shouldn't be. Unfrazzle must be part of everyone's everyday in order to feel calmer and happier inside.

> **Part 1:** *Over the next day or so, notice what routines in your life cause frazzle – whether it's the way they're done, or the way they are. There's no need to change anything right now – acknowledge, accept, and recognise that here is where it starts to get better. Make a list in your notebook of everything*

you do, whether it's something you enjoy or something you don't, whether small or big.

You only have two nervous systems – sympathetic and parasympathetic. You're either calm or not calm. So if an activity does not calm you down, it will be stressful, *even if you enjoy it.*

Don't show the results to anyone unless you really want to. Don't feel inhibited. And most of all, don't judge.

Part 2: *At the same time, notice any unfrazzling routines or habits in your life. Write these in another list.*

For example:

Frazzling routines & habits	Unfrazzling routines & habits
Using social media	Swimming
Checking emails	Yoga
Commuting	Reading
Getting kids ready for school	Singing
Food shopping	Walking the dog
Late nights	Gardening

When you've finished, look again at the first list. Are there any activities that could be non-frazzling – or even *un*frazzling – if you were able to do them differently?

Consider how you might change them. Make notes in your book as to how that might happen. This book is here to guide you through that.

Accepting the principles of Unfrazzle didn't mean my life changed overnight, but it was a first step in the right direction.

When I returned to the world, it was with an entirely new perspective.

Before the crisis, I'd found sanity in escaping into a world of make-believe. I still do: there's nothing more healing for me than using my imagination – whether in writing or reading fiction – to give me a mini-holiday in another world. When the crisis hit, the space I needed in order to be able to escape was severely affected. Writing fiction was no longer a safety valve, but another headbusting chore. But then I found an easier, more accessible route to calm, one that didn't involve me taking time out from the real world, but embracing the challenges within it.

I decided to use my everyday routines as opportunities to discover calm and space for myself. If commuting frazzled me, I would make commuting work in my favour instead. Rather than rushing through the everyday grind, I would reframe each element and turn it into an Unfrazzle opportunity instead.

As time went on, and as I transformed each routine, embedding them into my life, they became automatic behaviours. At the same time, much of what I'd previously thought of as important dropped away. Noticing 'wrongness' and 'rightness' became hugely unhelpful to my sense of calm. Being busy no longer seemed a badge of honour. I started to embrace wonkiness and accepting less than the best, and all of that came together into one complete plan to guide all the frazzled on the path to reclaiming true calm.

vi) How to keep positive

Exercise: Write a positive future

In your notebook, write a positive future for yourself, once you've completed the plan.

Specific future

Think of a situation you would like to deal with in a manner that helps you.

For example:

I would like to talk to my kids without losing my temper.

I would like to leave my phone in a drawer once a week.

I would like to get the headspace to read a book.

Wider future

Think of the perspective you would like to shift, the calm you would like to feel. Be grand. Go wild.

For example:

I would like to be a calmer, happier person.

I would like to not fear being bored.

I would like to not obsess so much about my so-called mistakes.

The symptoms of frazzle aren't nice. The endpoint of stress can be horrific. But the more we know, the more potential we have for change.

Go back to your list whenever you need a nudge back on the path towards Unfrazzle. Remember how good your future is going to be.

Once upon a time, I was so frazzled I could hardly think – and now everything has changed. Mental clarity and freedom is an amazing feeling: it will pull you back to the truly balanced person you are inside. And if I can change, so can you.

How to be you

I am writing this in the autumn of 2019, four and a half years after that photograph of me on my way to that Brighton Festival event was taken. Over time, my partner has made both small improvements and huge leaps forward – but also suffered setbacks too. It's by no means been a smooth trajectory – is anything in life, ever? – but with each bump in the road I've learned more about how to cope with the unexpected, helped by the journey I have been on.

I'd always imagined my desire for adrenaline was what made me feel alive. If I wasn't running late for appointments or packing my life full, then, I thought, I wasn't being me. What I'd never noticed was that the adrenaline rush was becoming triggered at ever more minor things. When I was in my twenties, I took myself off travelling and hardly turned a hair. In my forties, I was getting a rush of stress hormones at walking through the concourse of a busy railway station. And a brain adapted for frazzle was, as I learned the hard way, not doing me any good at all.

However, something else I discovered is that although the more we trigger stress, the worse it feels, the opposite is also true. The more I activate my parasympathetic response, the calmer I become. The calmer I become, the more brain space I find. The more brain space I have, the more I rediscover a me I long thought lost: the childhood me who drifted through life, never hurrying, never stressed, excited at the potential in each day. I would sit in my parents' garden, transfixed, as a bee buzzed about the lavender bush, feeling the sun warm on my head and the grass beneath my bare feet.

Decades later, I'm doing the same thing again: finding a stillness I didn't know was there. And that, I've realised, is the true me. Not just alive through adrenaline, but properly alive. Calmer, in balance, and able to relish the small things in life once more.

Another wonderful thing that's happened since beginning the journey of this book is connecting with all the many people who feel the same as I do: that despite the huge benefits of this era we live in, it is not serving us as it could. You'll meet some of these people in this book: they have done the exercises and given me their thoughts and feelings on how they're coping with twenty-first century life.

Let's not wait until our stress becomes so extreme we can no longer cope. The more work we can put in place before our crises hit, the better able we'll be to cope with them when and if they come. And if we're lucky enough never to go through a crisis, dialling down our frazzle is fundamental to being able to thrive in an imperfect world.

Therefore, if you feel the same way I once did, for whatever reason: stressed, overwhelmed, time-poor, fatigued, phone-addicted – or just simply with the feeling that *Life isn't right and I don't know why* – join all of us in this journey to thriving in the real world.

Chapter One summed up

- Learn your frazzle status. Knowledge is power.
- If you live through stress it will keep you low in every area of your life, damage your immune system, and lead to burnout.
- If things become unmanageable, turn to the extreme frazzle quick-fix spa retreat.
- The basic principles of Unfrazzle are: i) **Embrace imperfection** and ii) **Do less stuff.**
- Learn your frazzle values and watch them shift.
- Recognise what frazzles you, and consider the potential of change.
- Survival and healing comes from imagining a positive future, and then putting the steps in place to make that happen.

In a nutshell:

If you want to feel free from stress and overwhelm, start by recognising your frazzle

CHAPTER TWO

PHONE FRAZZLE: HOW TO TAKE CONTROL OF YOUR PHONE BRAIN

i) Ella and Ben

Ella

Ella is 26 years old, with jet-black hair and a face full of silver. She was a teenage skateboard champion, and now works as a sound technician, as well as making her own low-budget documentary films. She wants to change the world, is passionate about many things, and can often be seen on her BMX, weaving through the London traffic.

She carries her phone with her at all times. She needs it for work, for her out-of-work activities – and it's the main way she connects with friends. She would be lost without it. She has a presence on all the major networking sites, and uses them as part of her professional profile. She keeps her phone by her bed, and when she can't sleep – which is often – she'll scroll through her newsfeeds.

She says she's mostly healthy. She's vegan and tries to take care that she eats a balanced diet. Cycling is her exercise, and she thinks feeding the soul is an important part of health. When she can, she gets into the countryside, hooks up with close friends, sees her family, walks her parents' dog.

Ella has been suffering with anxiety since she was a teenager. Worries attack her, sometimes overwhelming her. There are times when she can't stop crying. She's had several panic attacks, some debilitating. On some days it's hard to drag herself out of bed. She sometimes feels as if she's living in a fog. She finds it hard to get her brain in order. She can't see her way out of this. She doesn't know what to do.

Ben

Ben is 45 years old, tall and angular. He wears small round glasses which make him look more serious than he is. He is sharply intelligent, and unexpectedly kind. He loves the south of France and dreams of living there one day. He has a dry sense of humour which not everyone gets. Despite appearances, he's rather absent-minded, and his expensive car is always a mess of smeared children's fingerprints, sweet wrappers and abandoned CD covers.

He's been a GP for nine years in a busy practice, and he finds his job fairly stressful. He feels he's sandwiched between patient needs, funding restrictions and NHS guidelines. His phone is with him at all times, partly as a necessity for his job, but also because he uses it to relax.

He reaches for it between patients to play a quick game, and uses it after work, including while sitting in his car in his driveway, before going into the house. He's been known to scroll through his phone on rare meals out with his wife. He gets up in the night and takes his phone with him to the bathroom.

Ben considers himself to have a healthy lifestyle. He loves running. He runs almost every day, and uses the time to clear his head. He doesn't smoke, and only drinks the odd glass of wine. He eats a home-cooked meal every night.

Ben is on anti-depressants, and takes sleeping pills inter-mittently. He's had sleeping problems for years. Despite his medical training, he suffers a lack of confidence in his memory. He often feels he has to check on the internet for health information he should already know.

His blood pressure is too high, he has palpitations, and he doesn't remember the last time he properly relaxed. He's cut down on coffee, but that hasn't helped. He finds it impossible to sit still for a moment. His wife comments on it, and he agrees – he's always telling his patients how bad stress is for their health. At the same time, he doesn't know what to do.

Ella and Ben's physical and mental health problems aren't caused by using their phones, but using their phones is making everything worse. Their addiction – and it *is* addiction – is frazzling their brain. It's doing so in a variety of ways, and is causing one or more of the following symptoms:

- a requirement for constant stimulation
- an exacerbation of any low feelings they already have
- ramped up stress and its consequences: (anxiety, insomnia, high blood pressure, inability to relax)
- a downgraded prefrontal cortex and hippocampus (a less-functioning 'clever' brain and a worse ability to remember)

In part **iv) How phones frazzle your brain,** you'll learn in more detail why that is so, and you'll get mini-exercises to help with each problem.

There are many theories as to why people nowadays are more stressed, anxious and sadder than they were before. All these theories may well be true. But phone addiction is petrol on the flames of mental ill-health.

Many of us who have ever reached compulsively for our phone have done so as distraction from problems and challenging emotions. But what we end up with are the symptoms of addiction, plus problems and challenging emotions. Managing phone use won't remove our challenges, but it will help with all those symptoms above. This is what getting control of your phone use will do for you:

- you'll feel calmer
- you'll be better able to cope with the lows
- you'll sleep better and relax more fully
- you'll have a better-working brain

This is entirely possible. It is possible for Ben and Ella, and it is possible for you. Even if you don't have a phone brain (see the quiz on the next page), you can access the benefits of being in control of your tech (as above), rather than vice versa. Total digital addicts – people worse than you – have learned how to manage their phone use and seen the results. You can do it.

ii) Quiz – Do you have a phone brain?

Read the descriptions below. (If you use your tablet or laptop instead of your phone, think about how you use that instead).

In your notebook, give yourself one point for all that apply. If your answer is 'sometimes', or 'occasionally', give yourself half a point.

1. I use my phone as an alarm clock.
2. I check my phone within fifteen minutes of waking.
3. I use my phone in bed at night.
4. I go on my phone if I am otherwise unoccupied, even for a moment.
5. I receive app notifications on my phone daily.
6. I check my emails three or more times per day.
7. I feel uncomfortable if I don't reply to emails immediately.
8. I use social media (whether reading or posting) every day.
9. I take part in string-texting (long back-and-forth texts or group messaging chats)
10. I spend at least one hour per day on social media.
11. I use my phone in the middle of the night.
12. I use my phone when I'm in the bathroom.
13. I use my phone while I'm eating meals.
14. When I'm with friends I'll read and reply to messages from other friends.
15. When I'm with friends I'll check social media on my phone.
16. I check emails after 9pm at night.
17. I check social media after 9pm at night.

18. I check my phone after 9pm at night.
19. I pick up my phone when I see it.
20. I check my phone while watching TV.
21. When I spend time with my family, I'll also be checking social media.
22. When I spend time with my family, I'll also be reading and replying to messages.
23. When I spend time with my family, I'll be using the internet by myself.
24. I feel uncomfortable if my phone isn't in the same room with me at all times.
25. I skim-read articles on my phone.
26. I don't watch to the end of videos on my phone.
27. I feel uncomfortable if I don't reply to text / other messages immediately.
28. I intend to use my phone for just a moment, and then lose track of time.
29. When I feel nervous or jittery, I reach for my phone.
30. I feel less confident in my judgement if I'm unable to check information on my phone.

Write down the total score in your notebook.

0 POINTS
Hooray! You don't have a phone brain.

1-10 POINTS
You don't have a phone brain, but you do feel compelled to use your device: I'll explain why that is so in the next section, **part iii.** This compulsive behaviour WILL frazzle your brain,

however rarely it occurs. If you want to unfrazzle your brain from your tech, try Method 1 in **part v** for How to take control of your phone brain. Implement the frazzle stops (in **part vi**) and the feel-good loop (in **part vii**) for when those behaviours emerge. The rest of the book will teach you how to prevent phone frazzle from occurring at all.

11-20 POINTS

You have a phone brain, but you have rules for when you won't use your phone. You're already trying to save your brain, and you're definitely able to take another step further. You've started to rewire your neurons, and in this chapter you'll learn how it's possible to do more. Try Method 2 for *How to take control*. The frazzle stop will be another tool in your armoury, as is the feel-good loop. In later chapters, you'll learn how to keep your phone in your bag, and continue on that path to true Unfrazzle.

21-30 POINTS

Your brain is phone-addicted, as are Ella's and Ben's, and millions of others. The definition of addiction is not only that the behaviour is compulsive, but that it also causes harm. In the next section, you'll learn how the brain becomes addicted, and the negative effects smartphone addiction has on the brain.

Rewiring takes time, but recognising and managing use is the first, vital step. Method 3 for *How to take control* may feel like a step too far, but think of it as an end goal, rather than an intermediate step. Go for Method 2 if that's the case. You'll need those frazzle stops while you're rewiring your brain, and learning the feel-good loop is essential.

My life as a phone addict

Some brains seem to be wired for phone addiction more than others – possibly due to an increased tolerance for dopamine (see **part iii**: *How smartphone addiction works* for more information on this). My brain is not as automatically wired for phone addiction as Ella's and Ben's. But phones are designed to be compulsive. Any human brain is capable of feeling that compulsion.

I resisted getting a smartphone for years. But in 2014, with my novel soon to be released, I was given an afternoon's training in how to use social media by my publisher – and a world I'd never understood before sprang to life.

I bought a phone, installed a few apps, and was soon as immersed as any other addict in the intense work of checking status updates, posting to my feed, liking, following, and all the rest.

Two years later, deep in the middle of crisis, I turned to social media more than ever, even though this time I hadn't the excuse of a novel to promote. It seemed a distraction from reality, and at the time I had no idea why, the more stressed I was, the more likely I was to flip to one of my apps. At the time, it seemed diverting to have my attention focused on other people's photographs, opinions, and messages.

And yet, every time I finally put down my phone, it was with a nauseous feeling, as if I'd just climbed off a merry-go-round. Time seemed to have slipped away from me, and I no longer knew where my head was. Stress continued churning through my body, and now, it appeared, I was also frazzling my brain.

When I belatedly came to the realisation that compulsively turning to my phone wasn't helpful in my search for calm, I turned to all-out war. I deleted all my apps and came off social media for months. I stopped checking emails for a couple of weeks, and the only reason I used the internet was to stream a film. No more researching, no more fact-checking – it was what's often called a digital detox.

Can you guess what happened?

That's right: it didn't work.

The moment I went back to my phone, I was as drawn in as ever. Social media was just as compulsive and checking emails gave me the same reaction as before. Sure, a digital detox helped while I was actually *doing* it. But the whole point of a detox is that you feel better afterwards as well. With compulsive behaviours, that just doesn't add up.

I had a choice: never use a smartphone again (see Method 3 in **part v** for how to do this), or severely restrict my phone use. Firstly, I came up with frazzle stops to prevent me picking up my phone (see **part vi** in this chapter). Then I chose a management plan. You'll discover the options for these in **part v**.

That was the start of getting back control of my brain, but it wasn't the end. Doing the other exercises in the plan – for sleep, blank time and reconnection (in Chapters Three, Four and Five) was what fundamentally helped to rewire my brain away from compulsivity towards my phone.

So even though I'm not as naturally drawn towards phone addiction as others might be, social media affects my brain just the same as it does other people's. In the next part, you'll read how addiction works on the brain, and exactly what smartphones do (warning: it'll make you see them in a whole new light).

We're all capable of using our phone as a distraction: via games, messaging, social media, web searches – whatever. It's our phones we turn to because what they contain is compulsive and never-ending. We tell ourselves they are useful. But managing my phone use was hands down the clearest way to stop frying my brain.

iii) How to get a phone brain

Your brain is plastic. It is malleable, and it is constantly changing. Your earliest experiences, and the stimuli you're exposed to throughout your life, spark neural connections. If you repeat and reinforce those connections, you'll rewire your brain, creating automatic responses to certain triggers.

I love bookshops and libraries. It doesn't matter whether I'm in a tiny independent or a huge chain store; if I'm surrounded by books on shelves I feel calmer and happier. I wasn't born that way; it's because I made the connection *books on shelves = reading = pleasure* at an early age, when my brain was more malleable. Unintentionally, I reinforced that connection over and over until my response became automatic.

That's because if our brain fires two neurons at the same time, repeatedly, they are both more likely to stick. This is to do with association. This works for any area of the brain, including memory and emotion. If you had a blissful holiday in Dorset one summer, whenever you think of that beach in summer, you'll associate it with happiness.

It also works with habits and routines. If we decide that the moment we wake up we will meditate for three minutes, with enough practice our brain will associate *morning* with *meditation*. Once the routine is embedded in the brain it will become almost automatic.

About neurons & neurotransmitters

Neurons are brain cells that use electrical charges to transmit information. Neurons have a control centre (the soma), branches (dendrites), and a chute (the axon), along which the information travels.

There are two types of neurons: those that send the charge (pre-synaptic), and those that receive it (post-synaptic). When stimulation activates the pre-synaptic neuron it sends a chemical called a neurotransmitter towards the receiving neuron: that's a synapse.

Some important neurotransmitters for frazzle and Unfrazzle include:

- Adrenaline (which also acts as the *fight-or-flight* hormone)
- Dopamine (often known as the motivational or reward chemical)
- Serotonin (often known as the happy chemical)
- Endorphins (pain-relievers and euphoria boosters)

… and you'll hear more about all of these later in this chapter.

However, through those automatic responses, rewiring can also create neurological dependencies and addictions. It's the methodology behind any brain-based part of addiction (as opposed to a social dependency, for example). For example, if we smoke a cigarette when we wake up every morning for a week, our brain will rewire to associate *waking up* with *smoke a cigarette.* Our neurons have fused in a new way.

Addictive behaviours take very little reinforcement for a rewiring of the brain to take place. In addition, many substances are in themselves addictive (nicotine, for example).

Psychiatrist and writer Norman Doidge defines addiction as having a wider scope than only drug or alcohol addiction.

'People can be seriously addicted to gambling, even running,' he writes in his investigative book into brain plasticity, *The Brain That Changes Itself*:

> *"All addicts show a loss of control of the activity, compulsively seek it out despite negative consequences, develop tolerance so that they need higher and higher levels of stimulation for satisfaction, and experience withdrawal if they can't consummate the addictive act."*

Sound familiar? Have you seen a smartphone addict literally unable to put down their device for more than a few minutes, fearful at leaving the house without it, frantic if it's been lost? Have you also heard them acknowledge the consequences of overusing phones, yet been unable to stop? Do they make up excuses as to why having their phone with them is necessary? Is that person you?

We don't know – as yet – of the precise health implications of smartphone addiction. But the early signs are not good.

The pleasure pathways of the brain

You might have heard about the neurotransmitter dopamine, and its connection to addictive behaviours. In fact, dopamine is necessary for mammalian survival. Without it we would be entirely lacking in motivation. It gets us out of bed in the morning, for without dopamine, we would take no pleasure in life.

This is because dopamine is anticipatory; it's a message that if we do *X,* we'll get a rush of bliss, a pleasure hit. *X* might be eating a delicious meal, or finishing a set task. The pleasure we get comes from endorphins and other feel-good chemicals. This is the brain's pleasure system, and it is what makes us feel properly alive, rather than just existing.

Dopamine is often called the reward neurotransmitter. It's a buzz that says *You got this! You're doing it!* It's a great sensation, because humans like rewards, and each one we receive makes us want another. Rewards aren't necessarily addictive – that depends on which activity the dopamine is based.

Example 1

Nav goes to a party, hoping she might bump into Jem, who was there last week (search for pleasure). At the party, Nav searches the room, and gets a mini-thrill when she sees Jem (dopamine + bliss chemicals = pleasure hit). Jem catches her eye (hit) and smiles (hit). Nav walks towards Jem, who turns to talk to her (hit). They chat, and then Nav tentatively asks, 'Fancy swapping phone numbers?' Jem grins. 'Great idea!' (hit). At the end of the night, Nav and Jem share a kiss (big rush of pleasure).

Each hit of pleasure, signalled by dopamine, makes Nav want more until the final big rush arrives.

Example 2:

Simon comes home, hungry, to the scent of onion and garlic frying in a pan (anticipation = dopamine release). He sits at the table and eyes his plate of pasta and tomatoes with anticipation – his favourite meal (anticipatory dopamine). He twirls pasta onto his fork and lifts it to his mouth, breathing in the smell of the meal (dopamine). He puts it in his mouth and tastes it – delicious (mini-pleasure hit). He eats the meal and feels full and satisfied (final rush of pleasure).

Why phones trigger dopamine release

We achieve mini-hits of pleasure in the completion of tasks. If you've ever taken joy in ticking items off your 'to-do' list, that's your brain firing anticipatory dopamine and releasing mini-endorphins when the tasks are done. Phones offer the same potential for pleasure hits – or so the brain believes.

Example 3:

Katy's on the way to the bus stop when she hears her phone beep (a task to complete = dopamine release). Once at the bus stop, she swipes to open her phone and sees she has a new email (reading = another task to complete = dopamine release). She reads the email – a bank statement to open and save on the cloud (another task = dopamine release).

She clicks on a social media app – 25 notifications (brain prepares for tasks = dopamine release). Some are likes and comments on her last post, a cute photo of her cat. Some are new followers, some are posts the app thinks she might be interested in. Katy's brain sifts and sorts for tasks: to follow back, to reply to the comment, to like a post on her feed (dopamine/dopamine/dopamine).

On the bus, she spots a highlighted link to a news item someone's posted – she feels the need to check it out (task = dopamine). Scanning the item for more tasks (dopamine), she spots an interesting link and clicks to find out more (task = dopamine). She pulls up a game on her phone – it requires spotting, sorting and quick reflexes (tons of tasks = tons of dopamine).

How using our phone leaves us always wanting more

Katy's brain might imagine pleasure will follow the likes, the follows, the points and the information, but that's a myth. In fact, she has zero chance of achieving pleasure – even though it's what she – and all of us – are ultimately looking for. Bliss comes from satisfaction – the satiation after a good meal, the feel-good chemicals that flood Naz's body after her kiss with Jem. It can even come after you've ticked all the items from your 'to-do' list, or finished that tricky crossword in the newspaper. It's that happy sensation after the completion of a set task.

When you use your phone, your brain sees a bundle of tasks to complete (emails, texts, other notifications), and a flood of potential bliss to follow, but that's a myth. Your brain has zero chance of achieving true pleasure from feel-good chemicals: all it will get is a list of dopamine-based tasks that never ends, and potential bliss that never comes.

This isn't your fault: creators of social media apps have admitted, even been proud of, the way they harnessed the brain's requirement for dopamine to ensure compulsive, addictive behaviours around phone use. As a very basic equation, addiction = profit. And an addiction that is normalised in society (we tend to accept people bent over their phones, tapping and scrolling) = even greater profit.

Tolerance & cravings: How smartphone (and any other brain-based) addiction works

Remember Ben, the GP from the start of the chapter? He loved his first smartphone, back in 2008. The novelty of it was a real kick, and he adored playing with it and its potential.

Over time, the novelty wore off – and so did his enjoyment. He can't even say he likes using his phone any more, although he uses it more than ever.

It wasn't just lack of novelty that dampened his enjoyment. Addictive substances – whether that's alcohol, heroin or smartphones – have the potential to flood the brain with dopamine, overwhelming the neurons that receive it. As a survival mechanism, the brain 'turns down' the effect of the dopamine. In other words, Ben's brain is getting more dopamine than ever before, but without feeling the full effect of each motivational kick.

Consequence: Ben's brain needs more dopamine to get the same buzz he used to get. It's why a hardcore gambler can spend all night at the tables in the casino, chasing the dopamine kick they used to have after winning one round of pontoon.

Tolerance means the brain adapts to its flood of dopamine. And what happens then is that the addict gets intense cravings.

Ella feels lost without her phone. She panics if she leaves it behind. She cradles it in her hand, like a pet. That's because her brain is so tolerant to dopamine – which has also disrupted her emotional brain – it now needs her phone just to feel normal.

It's the equivalent of an alcoholic who drinks a bottle of whisky that would floor another person. They're in search of the warm, fuzzy feeling that used to come after a couple of glasses of wine.

Neuroplasticity: the good news

Luckily, most people are not born addicts. It's our plastic, constantly changing brain that has the ability to create addictions via new neural pathways, repeated and reinforced.

In the same way, the brain has the potential to drop those addictions too. If a pathway is neglected and never reinforced through repetitive behaviour, the brain's automatic reaction will also change.

That's easier when we're not addicted. But we all know hardcore smokers who've given up the fags and never gone back. We also know people who've given up and restarted – because their brain wants to go back into its well-worn grooves.

Smartphones, right now, are often seen as a necessity. But once upon a time, so were cigarettes (doctors even recommended them for health). In the following section, you'll learn what smartphone addiction does to the brain – but keep in mind that change is possible. Knowledge is power.

iv) How phones frazzle your brain

a) Phones make your brain seek constant stimulation

In many ways, digital addiction works on the brain in the same way as any other addiction. However, it is also unique, because the digital world offers us a smorgasbord of choice, and so our task-reward-pleasure system will never be truly fulfilled. With many addictions that have a physiological element, there is the point of no beyond – the body ensures it.

But the digital world never ends. It is infinite, and we always want more, and so activates the dopamine pathway again and again. This remaps the brain to seek instant pleasure where it can.

When we're phone-addicted, we can get dopamine more quickly than ever – and so, because of tolerance and cravings, that no longer becomes enough for our brain. It needs more dopamine, and then yet more.

We have remapped the brain so it sees the world in a digital-like way. The digital world is very stimulating for our brains – it's uptime, not downtime. One consequence of this remapping is that the brain literally cannot bear to be bored. It fears under-stimulation as never before. The brain needs to be kept occupied at all times, despite its owner's best intentions. We can end up viewing the world as a vending machine – or as a giant phone.

Mini-exercise

Can you remember the two basic principles of Unfrazzle? Think about how they apply to smartphones and the need for constant simulation.

Follow the two principles, and you'll see that smartphones are useful, but useful like a crazed guard dog we own might be: a beast that we use to our advantage, but over whom most of us have very little control.

b) Phones make our brain sad

Too much dopamine in the brain affects our mood, cognition and motor skills. That's partly because in a healthy brain there's a fine balance of chemicals, including serotonin, the happiness neurotransmitter, and endorphins, which relieve pain and boost pleasure. Any imbalance in our brain can upset these levels.

As recent studies are starting to show[3], there is now a proven link between smartphone addiction and depression. And although these are extreme cases, it's certain that over-using your phone will impact, inevitably, on your ability to feel happy. If you're suffering mental ill-health, it's why you may feel worse after using your phone (as did I): imbalanced brain chemistry.

Mini-exercise:

Write or think of **five** activities that give you a mini-hit of pleasure (those that leave you with a feeling of satisfaction). These must be **non-phone based**. For example: cooking a meal I like / singing a song / weeding the garden / meeting a friend / completing everything on my to-do list.
When doing this, **immerse yourself in pleasure**. Really

---

3   https://www.ncbi.nlm.nih.gov/pmc/articles/PMC5970452/

feel the bliss-hits you get. Enjoy them. Notice how real these are, as opposed to the non-pleasure from phone use.

c) Phones make our brain stressed

That constant stimulation prevents the brain from getting its necessary rest. Every brain needs some downtime. Without downtime the brain can't find its off-switch. Without a chance to recharge, your brain becomes stressed.

There is no such thing as 'good' or 'bad' stress; it will affect your body in the same way. Even when I thought my phone was brilliant, and mostly harmless, using it was still stressing my brain.

Stress activates the body's sympathetic, fight-or-flight nervous system, and causes a rush of cortisol and adrenaline. Your heart rate speeds up, you become short of breath, and you get a spike in blood sugar. This is true whether you enjoy your stress, are neutral, or hate it.

A constantly-activated stress response is something anyone can get used to. You might not notice that going online spikes your stress. But you'll notice its consequences: poor sleep, anxiety and overwhelm, fatigue, blood sugar instability, and many more.

You can experience stress from many causes. Phones won't be the entire cause. However, managing use is vital to dialling down your total stress load.

Mini-exercise

How many apps do you have on your phone? Try to recall them now, and think of the least-frazzling 20% – ones that have a finite amount of dopamine hits you can receive. Mine are a weather app and a train times app. They don't offer a rabbit hole of possibilities, and have a highly specific use. What are yours?

Retain this information: you'll use it in the *How to take control* methods of managing phone use.

d) Phones make our brain stupid

There are several broad areas of the brain, which in general take on separate tasks. One is the frontal lobe. Its existence distinguishes us from the apes, and within that is the prefrontal cortex that controls our so-called 'clever brain'; our higher thought processes – logic, sequencing, planning, decision making, attention. These processes are severely affected by brain frazzle. Another part of the brain contains the temporal lobes, which house the memory area of the brain, known as the hippocampus.

Both memory and intelligence are affected by compulsive, repeated smartphone use. Partly it's because (as I mentioned earlier), the brain's pursuit of desire via the first pleasure system means that phones have remapped the brain to seek instant gratification. In other words, it's become lazy – and using the clever brain or retrieving information from memory requires work.

In addition, many of the tasks the brain usually undertakes have been outsourced to search engines, digital calendars, and more. We no longer need our memory to be as sharp, because our phone is always there to remind us of our appointments, and to tell us how to do things we've already learned. We don't need to use the critical faculties in our clever brain, because our phone will provide us with a précis of current thinking on the matter. It will think critically for us. Research becomes easy, because a search engine does the work.

If you don't exercise any area of the brain, those neuronal connections will start to wither. In the worst case scenario, they fall away. Ben's brain is lazier and more stupid than when he left medical school – not because he's older, but because he's allowed once-strong connections to weaken through lack of practice and repetition. He's not working his brain; he's relying on his phone.

On the other hand, it's within his power to strengthen those neglected pathways – and in fact, to have a sharper brain than he's ever had in his life. If you find it harder to remember your schedule than before, or if you find making decisions and using logic trickier than you used to, remember that this is not inevitable. You can stop the rot. This book will show you how.

Mini-exercise

How lazy has your brain got? In *Phones make your brain seek constant stimulation*, I asked you to remember the two basic principles of Unfrazzle. Did you
a) remember them without having to check?
b) flip back to check?
c) not even bother to answer the question?

If you answered c), see if you can remember them now. Why? Because working the brain exercises the neurons. The lazier the brain, the harder the exercise feels. But ultimately, hard work = greater brain benefits.

Later in the book, you'll find tips and exercises for working the brain. In effect, every exercise here will work your brain in a new way. This book will stop you being stupid.

Detention stories – Anthony

Anthony is 37 years old, with a master's degree, and is fluent in six languages. He is a calm, thoughtful person and takes time to speak to the new arrivals in order to settle them and help them where he can.

One of the centre rules is that no smartphones are allowed. On entry, the residents are permitted to borrow a standard cheap phone to make calls and send texts. The internet can be used in the library, but most sites are blocked, and the connection is in any case extremely slow.

One day, we talk about this in class. 'You know, I never thought this would be a good thing,' Anthony says. 'Not to have my phone. But I realise how much I use it to look up all my information.'

The rest of the class disagree vehemently. But Anthony is insistent. 'I can call my solicitor and my family on this,' he says, gesturing with the cheap phone. 'What else do I need a phone for? I see all the young people using their phones and they don't use this.' He taps his head.

'Perhaps this is the only way in which detention has helped me,' he adds, to general disagreement from everyone else. 'We have to use our own thoughts and our own memories to learn.'

Remember: Dopamine without addiction is both pleasurable and harmless

Even though we're always searching for pleasure and satisfaction, dopamine – when not pursued to excess – is *not* harmful.

In fact, it's the neurotransmitter which drives us on to do great things, and even if it doesn't, it can still give you a great sense of fun and excitement.

This book will give you plenty of dopamine-based tasks to complete, quizzes to answer, and exercises to do. It aims to give you hits of harmless pleasure, unlike the endless tasks set by our phones.

v) How to take control of your phone brain

The clever and the emotional brain

Humans have a 'clever' brain and an 'emotional' brain.

The clever brain can choose to leave your phone alone. The emotional brain acts on instinct and compulsion. It literally cannot help itself.

The emotional brain is extremely powerful, much more so than the clever brain. It's why you'll reach for your phones when there's no real need. Your clever brain may justify this, but it's the emotional brain that's won.

How to beat the emotional brain – three methods

If you can create a pause for the emotional brain, your clever brain may have time to catch up, see the bigger picture, and make an informed decision over whether it's necessary to check your emails right now. Remember, the emotional brain, acting on impulse, wants to go on social media, check its notifications, play another level. The clever brain knows that to unfrazzle, it needs to manage its phone use.

The longer the pause between impulse and acting on it, the more chance the clever brain has of catching up. Once you realise that it's a compulsion controlling you, you may decide to take charge. In time, you'll be able to change your relationship with your phone.

Method 1 (for non-addicts):
1. Open your phone and go to Settings.
2. Click on Apps.

3. Go through each app and untick the Show Notifications box apart from the one or two you deem 100% necessary (such as texts and other instant messages, perhaps).

4. Remember your 20% less frazzling apps? (The ones that are time and dopamine-limited, not endless). Remove all apps but these from your homescreen. That pause may be enough for you to think about whether you really need to be online.

Method 2 (for phone addicts):

1. Open your phone and go to Settings.

2. Click on Apps.

3. Think of your 80% most frazzling apps.

4. For one week, give yourself an app holiday. Uninstall **all** of the most frazzling apps.

5. If you need to access any of these sites, do so via the web. Typing details into your login page may give your clever brain time to catch up and decide if it really wants to be on its phone right now.

6. If you decide to reinstall your apps, it's easily done via the usual page. But see how long you can last before you do that.

Method 3: the ultimate challenge

Jo is a mental health nurse. She has two teenage children and a demanding job. In other words, she's always busy. This is what she says about managing her tech use.

"I have what I call a 'dumbphone' – basically a brick – and a tablet. Doing this enables me to prioritise areas of my life, so I use my brick phone at work, and my tablet at home. I divert my phone to voicemail when I'm at home, but it remains switched on, so I can be contacted in an emergency.

I try my hardest to stay focused at work, and rarely make personal calls or emails during working hours. Equally, when not at work I switch off my work devices and set out-of-office automatic replies. This means that I can separate the use of social media and internet for leisure at a specific time that suits me.

The only downside I've found to not having a smartphone is that people keep asking me to use messaging platforms like WhatsApp. But I prefer not to be expected to be constantly, and instantly, available."

How to trial this

If you already have a tablet, buy a cheap non-smartphone. Send a message to your instant chats groups that you're taking a chat holiday for a few days. Transfer your SIM card to your new phone, and use it only for texting and calling. Then see how often you can leave your tablet at home when you go out of the house.

vi) The frazzle stop

Sometimes, however, that pause won't be enough. Even after uninstalling your most toxic social media apps, there will still be times when stress hormones are racing round your system, and you'll find yourself picking up your phone.

The best way to tackle this is to keep a 'frazzle stop' handy for those times when you'd otherwise be scrolling through newsfeeds, or whatever else you might do.

A frazzle stop won't *un*-frazzle your brain. You'll layer up Unfrazzles in Chapters Three to Six – but before that, let's stop things getting worse. That's what these quick fixes will do for you.

Below is a list of fifteen frazzle stops. You'll have others that will be personal to you. Each task must give you harmless dopamine hits of pleasure. The best way to do this is with an activity that keeps your hands busy (because your fingers and thumbs are brain-mapped for swiping and scrolling through phone screens, and so they'll be itching to move). It must also be focused on mini-rewards.

You cannot start to unfrazzle without learning to put down your phone, and so a frazzle stop must be a quick fix, available **immediately,** that will feed the desire for easy pleasure in a neutral (or beneficial) way. It will distract your brain with a finite, limited choice. It's a necessary step on the path to taking back control.

Personally, I travel with a page-turner of a novel in my bag, and I keep a magazine nearby that I can pick up when I would otherwise be on my phone. We're all different: do something that works for you. It should be **tactile** (involving your hands) and must keep your **brain** occupied.

Exercise: pick your frazzle stop

In your notebook, write any **frazzle stops** that you're willing to try during the next few weeks. Choose from the list below, or think of your own. Choose ones that are available to you immediately, or almost immediately. If you've never knitted, but you'd like to, put it into your long-term plan (as you'll read below, it can be a brain-saver). You must already have the basic rudiments of the skill, and access to materials (there's no point choosing gardening if you don't have access to a garden). It should be something that you can do when the urge to go online strikes you immediately.

newspapers
magazines
information leaflets
puzzle books
quizzes
colouring-in
novels
non-fiction books
knitting, sewing or crocheting
gardening
household chores (seriously!)
musical instrument
model-making
jigsaws
patience card games

Over the next few days, see if you can add any more to your list.

Christine is the editor of a national magazine. Below is her own frazzle stop, which works so well it's become her full-time job.

I learnt to knit as a child but didn't take it up as an everyday hobby until I took a stressful job on an international newswire in Vienna. Working in shifts and being on call at odd times of day or night made me feel tense and anxious, and I struggled to sit still in front of the TV and relax during my evenings off. At the same time I was a long way from all my family and didn't have friends to go out for drinks with to ease the tension.

One day, passing a local wool shop, I was drawn to a soft ball of yarn and, thanks to the helpful owner, soon found myself with wool and needles in hand. Not only did the rhythmic movement of knitting and the comforting feeling of soft yarn passing through my fingers soothe my nerves, but I also found that while my hands were occupied I was distracted enough from my worries to watch TV and wind down in the evenings. Knitting gifts also helped me feel closer to the family and friends I'd left behind in the UK.

I've been knitting regularly ever since then, and a few years ago combined my experience in journalism with my love of crafts by taking a job as editor of a monthly knitting magazine. Now I'm a busy mum of two working four days a week in a fairly demanding role, and I knit to relax almost every day. I also love knitting on journeys, and recently was able to defuse an impending panic attack on a flight by distracting myself with knitting. I rarely reach for my phone in the evening as my hands are full of wool!

vii) The feel-good loop

Those of us who have ever suffered anxiety will know this thought-chain well:

"I still feel anxious and stressed" ⟶ "I'll check my phone" ⟶ "I still feel anxious and stressed" ⟶ "I'll check my phone" ⟶ "I still feel anxious and stressed." ⟶ "I'll check my phone" ⟶ "I STILL feel anxious & stressed"...

It's inevitable that at some point, and however committed you are to rescuing your brain from frazzle, you'll go to your phone. I've told you that my phone distracted me when I was anxious and stressed – and it left me more anxious and more stressed. It's so important that nobody feels bad for doing this. We are all only humans, with human brains.

If you're committed to taking control of your brain, and if you recognise the feel-bad loop, then replace it with the feel-good loop below. And remember – we've all been there...

Exercise: The feel-good loop

Choose one or more of the following statements to repeat to yourself, whenever you find yourself mindlessly trawling through your phone:

I recognise that this isn't helping my brain.
I know this is hard.
I am doing well.
There is no such thing as a mistake.
*Rewiring the brain takes **time**.*

Creative mindfulness writer and teacher **Wendy-Ann Greenhalgh** regularly uses social media to post mindfully on her creative projects, and the images and thoughts that inspire her. Here are her tips for using social media:

- Don't allow push notifications for anything. If you don't know there's chocolate in the fridge then you won't want to eat it!
- Notice your emotional and mental responses in the moment, as you're scrolling or logging on, so you know if they're becoming compulsive or unmindful.
- Only follow people who inspire you.

Chapter Two summed up

Addiction

- Brain plasticity can work to create both good habits and harmful addictions.
- Brain-based addiction and its consequences are formed when the brain craves ever more dopamine.
- Addiction means we get cravings for more of the drug, but with constantly reduced pleasure.

Phone addiction

- Phone addiction frazzles us in four major ways:
- It makes our brains seek constant stimulation.
- It makes us sad.
- It makes us stressed.
- It makes us stupid.
- Dopamine-based pleasure is not harmful in itself. It can give us a great sense of feeling alive.

Practical steps

- Take an app holiday. Creating a pause for the emotional brain allows your clever brain to catch up.
- Choose your frazzle-stops. They will give your hands and brain something to do instead of scrolling or swiping.
- When you mindlessly use your phone, acknowledge that, without judgement.

Remember:

You **can** rewire your brain away from compulsions.
You **can** take back control of your brain.

In a nutshell:

If you want to stop feeling over-frazzled right now, leave your phone and other devices alone.

CHAPTER THREE

THE WIND-DOWN ZONE: HOW TO SLEEP WELL

Do you ever wish you could carve out a nurturing evening for yourself? In the hour or so (perhaps more, perhaps less) before you go to bed – a space where you can be free of the pressures of the day, when you can curl up with a book or a film, or listen to an album. Perhaps you'd love a scented candlelit bath, or just to sit by a window and watch the evening pass by.

Yet when the opportunity presents itself, it often doesn't work out as you hoped. You plan for your bath, or your book, and then life seems to get in the way. The kids demand too much of your time and attention. There's a work email that needs replying to. The washing up won't do itself. Your housemate has invited a load of friends back. Your teenage daughter is out late and hasn't answered your text. You can't switch off your brain from its usual routes.

Even when you manage to plug in the time, it's never quite as you wanted. It's hard to let go and exist in the moment. The bath isn't the right temperature. There are wet towels on the floor. There's no film you feel like watching, no album that matches your mood. In fact, all you want to do is collapse into bed – and yet when you're there, you struggle to sleep as restfully as you'd like.

This chapter will give you back your evening downtime. It will lay the foundation for a restful night's sleep – which doesn't start the moment you get into bed, but much earlier.

This important step in unfrazzling will give you an hour or so to unwind before bed.

In this chapter, you'll learn how to activate the 'off' switch. It starts by following the two principles of Unfrazzle:

Embrace imperfection

Do less stuff

The bath, the TV programme, the book – none of these will be right, and it won't matter. Life will get in the way, and that won't matter. By embracing imperfection and doing less stuff you will unfrazzle, no matter what.

By the end of this chapter, you will have learned:

- how lack of sleep frazzles, and how frazzle causes lack of sleep.
- easy tips and tricks to get yourself a better night's sleep.
- how *The Wind-Down Zone* works to nurture your downtime and reset your brain.
- more on the power of routines.
- step by step exercises to unfrazzle and unwind with time to yourself before bed.

i) How do you sleep?

How do you sleep?

At different times of your life you'll sleep better or worse than you do now. But sleeplessness is almost bound to affect you at some stage. Last month things may have been different, and next month they may well be different again. But thinking about the past fortnight, read the four statements below.

Which statement do you agree with, *as your life is right now?*

- *Most days, I sleep soundly throughout the night and wake feeling refreshed.*
- *I feel as if my sleep is OK, but I regularly wake feeling as if I haven't had enough, and throughout the day I can't seem to shake it off.*
- *I struggle to fall asleep and/or I often wake in the night. I have a few tricks that send me back to sleep. I'll be exhausted the next day, but that's life.*
- *It takes me a long time to fall asleep and/or when I wake in the night, it can take me ages to fall back. If it's late enough I won't be able to fall asleep at all. I only seem to do that when it's time to get up.*

Sleep heals. It's vital for our mental wellbeing: as neuroscientist Matthew Walker writes in *Why We Sleep*, it enhances *all* of our brain processes if we can get enough of it, and impairs them all if we don't. However, you won't need a scientist to tell you that: if you've ever dragged yourself through the day, muddle-headed, wired on caffeine, unable to remember which way is up, you'll know what happens to your brain after lack of sleep.

So how do you go about getting a decent night's rest? Go online and you can find dozens of methods claiming to help you sleep. Plenty of 'sleep experts' claim to have found the magic formula. In reality, there are countless reasons why people don't sleep, yet only around a dozen common-sense tips that will help to nudge your advantage. At the end of this chapter, I'll list them. Even small changes can have huge benefits, so try the ones that make sense and see what works.

However, there is one broad, fundamental reason as to why people don't sleep, and it is this: **stress.**

Stress can be physical *or* emotional. If your body is processing stress from *any* source, it will be harder to sleep.

Whether you're worrying about your job, or if you've drunk too much and you're brewing a hangover (or both), the stress on your body means you won't sleep.

Stress can even remain inside the body once its original source has gone. Our brain, our endocrine (hormone) system, our guts – they can remain in a stressed state from incidents of years before.

Cat is a musician. She has had insomnia for around thirty years and would agree with the fourth statement on the list above.
Between the ages of nine and fourteen I lived in an eccentric Brighton hotel that was owned by a local gangster. The clients were a real mix – holidaymakers, businessmen, criminals, and many 'lost' people of the world.
It was a fun, exciting life and I was totally free to do what I wanted. I used to sleep wherever I felt like it, many times on a bed beside the night buzzer. If a guest forgot their

key they would ring the bell and I would jump out of bed and run to let them in. I was also often woken up by some big drama – for example when the hotel next door caught fire, the owner rang the night buzzer, and my sister and I had to wake everyone up to evacuate the hotel.

Another time it was rung by people coming from the Grand Hotel on the seafront. It had been bombed by the IRA during the Conservative Party Conference in 1984 and I was asked if our family would open the doors to the evacuated guests. I remember my family making them fried egg sandwiches and lending them the hotel phone to call their families. One overheard conversation sticks in my memory: 'Hello, it's Mummy here. Don't panic – Maggie's all right. Yes – and your father's fine too.'

Those five years – as exciting as they were – had a profound impact on me. My life in the hotel had a lasting effect on my ability to relax at night time, even though it happened so long ago. Over time, my heightened awareness at night developed into long-term insomnia. Basically, even though I've tried every trick in the book, I can't properly relax until around 6am, or when the sun comes up.

That's because somewhere in my unconscious, my brain thinks it has to be on alert during the night in case anything happens. In addition, if someone knocks or rings on the door when I'm in bed, I leap faster than Usain Bolt to answer it. That's because it's a direct link to the sound of the hotel night buzzer. Once I realised why I couldn't sleep, I could take action to fix it. I went from building a lifestyle around insomnia to taking steps to reprogramme my sleep responses. It's working; things are getting much better.

Do you match the fourth statement on the list, like Cat? Do you suffer insomnia even though there is no obvious cause?

If your body is holding on to tension – even though it may be stress from decades before – it can be extremely difficult to let go enough in order to sleep.

In addition, if you're going through stress now – whether physical or psycho-emotional – your sleep-wake cycle will be disrupted. Even if the cause of stress is not linked directly to the night-time, it can still cause insomnia.

Detention stories – Oscar

Oscar, a softly-spoken 22-year-old who loves music and dancing, has been in the detention centre for two months. At the beginning, he made an effort to turn up to the classroom at nine in the morning, but as time's gone on he's looked more and more exhausted: he's struggled to respond when he's spoken to, and appears to be in a daze. Currently, he sleeps until around eleven, and turns up in the class at about eleven thirty.

'You just can't sleep in this place at night,' he tells me. There are the physical discomforts: the mattress and pillow are too thin, the air vent is directly over his head. There are three other beds in his small room – there are always residents leaving and arriving in his room, and sometimes they are moved there in the middle of the night.

Depending on who is currently residing in his room, some put the TV on until well into the early hours. Others drop in and out of each other's rooms and chat throughout the night or play cards. The corridor outside is alive with people hanging about, sometimes playing music, often talking on their phones.

Although initially he made an effort to get up at half past seven, just as he used to in his everyday life, and start his day as normal, the effect of only a couple of hours' sleep has started to take its toll. It now seems easier to do as most of the others are doing, and sleep between five and eleven.

'It's a coping strategy', he says. 'I'm under pressure, so I'll do what I can to get by: and if I can only sleep during the day, then that's what I'll do.'

Although there are natural 'night owls' – as well as 'morning larks' – most people fall into the middle, neither one extreme nor the other. It is not that night owls end up in detention, but that detention leads people to become night owls.

Why? Because stress disrupts the release of melatonin – the sleepy hormone – due to imbalanced levels of cortisol – the stress hormone. Stress causes the release of melatonin to push back to later and later on in the night, until – if you're suffering acute or chronic stress – you won't start to feel tired until daylight arrives, a complete topsy-turvy of how most people operate their everyday lives.

Our daytime and night-time instincts are primeval. In hunter-gatherer societies, the daytime is for chores, for being 'switched on'. The dark hours are when people gather to share stories, play music, laugh, relax, and switch off.

In addition, we are all more vulnerable at night. It is night-time when things can come to get us, and if we're stressed, we're on high alert, awaiting danger at all times. In detention, the danger that you'll be woken in the night with bad news is real.

It's therefore not surprising that when we are under stress, our brain prevents us from falling asleep at night.

One vital way to take yourself off high alert at night

It is very common – and seems to make sense – to use your phone as an alarm clock. It obviates the need to buy a separate device, for example. And we often believe we need to be immediately available at night – so that if a call comes with an emergency, we'll be there to answer it.

However, this is a 'need' that much of the time has been manufactured, stoked with the embers of latent stress. If some part of you feels you need to remain 'ready', you won't be able to relax enough to get that essential deep sleep, even if you're unconscious.

Your phone is designed to keep you on high alert. This is tricky enough in the daytime, but at night, if it lives by your bed it has the potential to disturb your sleep. Every time it pings or buzzes your brain will notice it, even if it doesn't properly wake you up. If you're phone-addicted, the temptation to pick it up if you can't sleep will be too strong if it's within grabbing distance.

You *must* be able to let go in order to get true, restful sleep. This is a quick fix, and although it's not the entire solution, it is a vital start.

Quick frazzle fix

Remove your phone from the bedroom at night

1. Do a mental search of your possessions.
2. Do you own an alarm clock? Ensure it works.
3. If not, do you own a spare mobile phone?

- Yes? Remove the SIM card and create a blank home screen. This will be your alarm.
- No? Buy an alarm clock **as soon as you can**. As a last resort, and in the meantime, use your mobile as your alarm.
- Put it **on flight mode** before you go to bed.
- Keep it as far from your bed as you can while still being able to hear the morning alarm.

In addition, tell everyone you can what you are doing and why. It will encourage you, and may help others not to try to contact you at night unless it's an emergency.

Are you the emergency contact for someone who may call you in the night? Download an app that will only allow specific numbers to be able to call or text you. Continue to leave the phone out of the room – on the landing maybe – with the ringer turned up.

Do you use your phone to write aides memoires? Keep a notepad by your bed. Scribble on to it and take the sheet with you when you get up.

Do you believe using your phone at night helps you to sleep? It doesn't. The blue light from the phone mimics daytime light, preventing the release of melatonin. The dopamine release from using your phone keeps your brain motivated and active. If you can't sleep and need distracting, look at the tips at the end of this chapter.

Belinda unfrazzles by playing the piano and growing plants on her roof terrace. She's a self-admitted phone addict.

I live upstairs from my 85-year-old father, and for this and many other reasons I often feel on 'high alert'. I've always kept my phone beside my bed in case any emergency calls came in during the night and I'm needed.

It's taken me ages to realise two things: firstly, that keeping the phone beside me was adding to my tension and unsettledness, and secondly, that I can't, and never will be able to catch any crises that come. It seems to me as if this need to be omnipotent will never end. A phone beside my bed isn't enough: in order to prevent any harm coming to my father I would have to follow him around 24/7, and even that wouldn't be adequate.

I've had to let go of that feeling, because I've realised that looking after my mental health was more important. I can't take care of my father, my mother or anyone else without it. It's why about four weeks ago I bought myself an alarm clock, installed it in my bedroom, and put my phone outside in the hallway at night-time. I have to accept that I can't stop anything bad happening, as much as I want it to.

I've already noticed the difference in my mental health. I sleep more soundly and when I wake up I feel so much better.

ii) Unfrazzle to sleep, sleep to unfrazzle

For many years before the crisis came, I used to wake up at half past six and commute to work in a haze of exhaustion. Sometimes I felt so tired I imagined dropping to the ground as I walked from the station every morning, and snoozing while people swerved around me. I dragged myself through the day, and so each night I tried to get eight hours sleep, but they never seemed enough. Ten hours would have been ideal, but that would have meant going to bed at eight thirty – it was never going to happen.

The crisis broke my life apart, and forced me to re-evaluate all my routines. I realised that for years I'd been living through frazzle. I packed my world with busy-ness and a desire to make perfect choices. In a buzzy, lively city where distractions abound and people always seem to be having a better time than you, it didn't occur to me that it was possible to say no, to do less, to embrace imperfection.

My evenings were a whirl of activity. I raced through my chores, and hurried through my bedtime routine so I could get under the covers by ten thirty with my chamomile tea. It didn't matter if I wasn't out partying every night – I was still *doing* stuff, and as a consequence my brain had no time off.

Time off for your brain is essential if you want to unfrazzle enough to get a good night's sleep. It is a virtuous circle, because a good night's sleep will, in turn, lead to Unfrazzle.

An overworked brain = frazzle

Imagine your brain is a secretary at a desk, and each piece of information arrives on that desk needing to be dealt with, and then filed. Imagine that desk covered with a teetering pile of stuff to be sorted, and as fast as it's sorted, yet more arrives.

Your secretary-brain needs time to get on top of things. It needs time when nothing else is incoming to process and file all that information. You don't know that it's doing it, because you're not conscious of all that filing and sorting occurring. But it's happening all the same.

In the two chapters that follow, you'll learn how to give your brain *deep time off* in order to truly unfrazzle. Each layer of time off will unfrazzle you further and further, and lead you towards getting a good night's sleep.

In other words, this chapter is not the only one that will get you to sleep. It is the start of sleep, not the end.

The brain is awake while asleep

Neuroscientist and sleep professor Matthew Walker explains that even during our deepest sleep, known as Stage 4 NREM (Non Rapid Eye Movement) sleep, the brain is hard at work. 'What you are actually experiencing during deep NREM sleep is one of the most epic displays of neural collaboration that we know of,' he writes in his comprehensive analysis of the subject, *Why We Sleep*. He likens the activity to a 'file-transfer process.' He continues, 'The state of deep NREM slow-wave sleep donates a state of inward reflection – one that fosters information and the distillation of memories.'

In other words, my brain needed time in order to sort and file the multitude of information it had received during the day. Teaching, commuting, writing – that's a lot of work for a brain to deal with. After work, my brain needed rest, so that it could resume all that filing and sorting with the energy it needs.

Because I was working my brain hard right up to bedtime, racing through my evening, I was giving it no down-time. Therefore, my brain had to sort through all that information at night. Even as I was unconscious, my brain was processing all the information it had received during the day.

Everyone needs time off for the brain. If you work your brain too hard during the daytime and evening, it can only process at night. And even if you're unconscious, your brain is actually awake.

That's because the brain is always active, even as the conscious mind switches off. After it's finished processing and sorting the major stuff, it goes into its optimal holding pattern of keeping you alive and fully rested. Your dreams are a part of the processing, but deep sleep is where your brain and body are refreshed. If you don't get enough, your brain will be overworked most of the night, doing the business it didn't get time to do in the day.

Dopamine frazzles our time off and prevents sleep

Dopamine is the task-and-reward neurotransmitter. It's essential to keep you alive and motivated. It's a 'wake up!' call to the brain – and your evenings should be 'wind down', not 'wake up' time.

Exercise: what's your evening frazzle?

Think back to what you know about dopamine (if you need a primer, turn to Chapter 2, *The Pleasure Pathways of the Brain* in part iii).

Now consider your time off before bed, your regular evening routines. How much dopamine do you pursue in the evening, *even when you're having a night in?* Think about where dopamine hits might be found, considering how much dopamine is offered by smartphones, tablets and other technology.

It's not only smartphones where evening frazzle can be found. Think about the principles of Unfrazzle and their opposite – pursuit of the optimum choice, constant busyness, trying to get it right, and so on.

What do you do, whether digital or non-digital, that stops your busy brain from resting as it should?

Write a list or a mind-map in your notebook, with the heading *MY EVENING FRAZZLE.*

Exercise – Jake and Aoife's frazzle factors

Now read about two people with ultra-frazzled evenings, Jake and Aoife. As you read, note the frazzle factors including dopamine hits anticipating pleasure, and whether they are under Jake and Aoife's control or not.

Also, consider whether there are any elements that are relevant to your life, and if you can add any more to the list you wrote in the previous exercise.

THE WIND-DOWN ZONE: HOW TO SLEEP WELL

Jake's evening

It's five-thirty in the evening, and Jake has just left work. He dodges traffic, the music blaring from shops and bars, car horns, cyclists, advertising hoardings, and newspaper vendors as he walks to the station.

The station is crammed full of people; a giant screen flashes out weather reports and celebrity news. Tannoy announcements boom of delays to places he's not going. People bump into him as he weaves along the concourse. He's offered a free cappuccino from a promo stand; he smiles briefly, shakes his head, moves on.

He waits with other commuters by the screens, and once his platform's announced, there's a surge through the barriers as everyone tries to get a seat by the window. Jake is amongst them, pushing forwards, hoping to get the seat he wants.

He succeeds, and the train moves off. He watches a box-set on his laptop and simultaneously flips to his inbox to catch up with emails. A notification from BBC news pings; he clicks on the link, posts it on Twitter, then plays a game on his phone, pausing his show.

Jake arrives home and dumps his stuff. As he's cooking his dinner his phone pings with messages, emails from work and social media updates. He scrolls through them all, ticking each one off his mental list. As he eats dinner he scrolls through news pages, then checks the weather for tomorrow on his app, then returns to Twitter to reply to comments on the link he posted.

After dinner he switches on the TV. There's a documentary he's been thinking about watching, so he puts it on, but it's not absorbing enough, and so he flips to another show. Maybe a film? He has a choice of several hundred on his streaming service. He scrolls through the list, finally chooses one, presses play. He really should get back to that work email, so he taps out a reply. Meanwhile someone posts in the messaging group he's part of, with a funny gif. He feels it's rude not to reply, and so he joins in the conversation. Then he checks his Twitter and Facebook newsfeeds while he has his phone in hand.

Nothing there, so he flips on Instagram. He's proud of only using Instagram in the evenings – he's seen other people use it all day! He taps a few likes, then goes to the toilet, taking his phone with him.

On the toilet he checks his notifications once more. Back in the living room, he has a WhatsApp message from a friend in another country – a pleasure he wasn't expecting. He reads it. They text back and forth for a bit.

When he looks up it's eleven o'clock and the film is still going; he's been half-watching it, double-checks the plot online, finds an interesting detail about the director and follows that link. Somehow, it's now ten to twelve.

Jake takes his phone to the bathroom as he brushes his teeth, then puts on his pyjamas and climbs into bed. He sets the alarm on his phone for the next day, then checks the weather again, and reads an interesting webpage before turning out the light. During the night, he can hear his phone vibrate on the bedside table as notifications come in, but finally he falls asleep.

He's woken by the alarm on his phone. And although he has been asleep – at least for some of the night – he feels as if he hasn't slept a wink.

Aoife's evening

Aoife is a mother of two. There is nothing she doesn't know about calm and wellbeing. Her living room is painted taupe because it's calming, and she keeps a variety of Ayurvedic spices in her kitchen cabinet. She has church candles on every surface, and she practises yoga and mindfulness daily.

Aoife spends hours cooking nutritionally balanced meals, and regularly hosts sleepovers for her children's friends. Her downtime belongs to her kids, searching the house for headbands and PE kits, helping them with homework, checking health information on the internet.

Life often feels frantic. When the children are in bed she cleans the house, does the washing and preps tomorrow's lunches. Exhausted, she compensates with a glass or two of wine, dazed in front of her laptop, and calls her sister to have a normal human to speak to.

Finally, she falls into bed at midnight, wired and wishing she could have just one evening alone to truly connect with herself.

Evening frazzle factors

In just one evening, Jake's brain is having to decode and process around 40 different visual and aural stimuli. Around 12 are not under his direct control (traffic, crowds, vendors, cappuccino-offerers), and these alone require a great deal of calm and headspace to negotiate.

The bulk of the stimuli is from his tech, and requires a vast amount of brain processing, not least because he jumps from one to the other and then back again (Twitter to news page to Twitter = 3 separate bits of stimuli). There are also often two or more bits of stimuli entering his brain at the same time (watching TV while texting a friend, for example).

On the other hand, Aoife's life is packed with constant busyness and a pursuit of perfection. She can argue until she's blue in the face how important it is to create nutritionally balanced meals, and I totally agree, but she never asks herself the question – which is more important? To be on the verge of breakdown, or to have all the correct nutrients in every meal? Only she can give that answer.

It's also Aoife's choice whether she wants to devote her evening to her children, or if she decides to carve out some space for herself within the chaos, whether she wants a lively, energetic but frazzling household, or a calmer, quieter but unfrazzled one.

These are difficult choices – but they are choices nonetheless. I used to think my frazzle was inevitable, and my evening routine was fine, until everything changed. Now I've realised that we can do less, and be imperfect, and that should be enough for me.

How I learned to sleep

During my high-achieving wellness journey I learned tons of stuff about sleep. I discovered the unlovely term 'sleep hygiene' (much of which has been distilled into the tips at the end of this chapter), and put every aspect in place. However, I came to realise – very slowly – that although learning about sleep waves and amber light, for example, was useful, there was one key trick that enabled me to have a restful night's sleep.

The answer was this: a low-impact, slow evening before bed. It didn't matter how imperfect that evening was; it was how I chose to go about my activities that held the answer. And as I pottered about the kitchen slowly cleaning up, a podcast burbling gently in the background, I found myself in a more natural rhythm, one I'd semi-forgotten.

You might live with other people who have a tendency to disrupt your calm. Perhaps you think your calm depends on theirs. But think of this the other way: if you can remain the still heart at the centre of the storm, you will impact on them as much as they on you.

Choose your own way of slowing your downtime. This chapter starts to unravel the stress of the day in the evening, and it is not an austere regime. This is about enjoying the darker hours, but in a calm, unfrazzling way.

Now, most days when I wake up, I feel refreshed. I go to bed tired and I sleep. If I'm frazzled, and I wake up with the old exhausted feeling, I know how to put the routines back in place in order to unfrazzle me once more. Now I have the key to sleep, I will never have a life of frantic evenings again.

iii) The power of routines

Routine (noun): A course of action to be followed regularly...; a set of normal procedures, often performed mechanically. Synonym: Rut.

[adapted from] https://en.wiktionary.org/wiki/routine

I've talked about routines as helping people to cope with the stress of detention. But they only began to release their true power when I devised a way to help us unfrazzle our brain for sleep.

Routines are often either taken for granted, or seen as dull. *My job's a bit routine, but it pays the bills.* Some people claim to despise routines – and yet, however much of a maverick we are, we have routines. Even people who have chosen to step outside society must, because they are human, have a routine – whether that's a routine of mind-bending drugs, or a walk to the local shop for milk and bread.

You might not relate routines to neurology. Yet routines create pathways in your brain. And because your brain is plastic, those pathways can change, as can your routines. Routines have immense power – to heal, to destroy, to give strength, to frazzle.

Evening routines are an opportunity to start your Unfrazzle. Think about Jake's evening, for example. At its basis, that routine is neutral and asymptomatic. He comes home from work, he makes his dinner, he has a few hours free after dinner, and he goes to bed. This is all pretty much non-negotiable. He *has to travel back from work, he has to eat, and he has to go to bed.*

Because your foundational routines are neutral (waking up, eating, brushing teeth, and so on), you have a choice. You can choose to use those routines as an opportunity for mini-retreats, to unfrazzle you. If you repeat routines in that way until they become a habit, then you will be rewiring your plastic brain to be calm. This will enable it to process the stimuli you've encountered throughout the day, and you'll be able to rest at night.

Here's another evening, based upon foundational routines.

Your bedtime story

It's seven in the evening. Earlier, you chose an album, and you're listening to it now as you cook. It's not the ideal music for your mood at that moment, but you don't change to another one. You turn down the volume.

As you eat dinner, you make a decision as to what you're going to watch tonight. After dinner, you switch on the TV and watch the programme from beginning to end. The show's OK; not ideal, but it doesn't matter.

You turn off the TV. You have a bath, then slowly get ready for bed and set the alarm on your clock for the next day. You climb under the covers and turn out the light.

You sleep.

When you marry routines with unfrazzling – doing fewer, less-than-optimum things, you'll have the potential to discover true, restful sleep.

You don't need the ideal life in order to sleep well. You don't need to create an Ayurvedic haven in your home, or paint the walls taupe. In fact, obsessing about getting everything perfect can have the opposite effect on your calm. Your mood music doesn't have to be the best ever, your evening entertainment can be 'that'll do'.

Life is often less than ideal. It is gritty, and mundane, and not quite a fairy tale. It's cold slices of toast and kids' muddy boots and a dog that's whining to be fed. It's a delayed train and no food in the fridge. It's a light that needs fixing and clothes that need ironing.

The thing is, however imperfect your daily life, you can still get a better night's sleep. You can wake, refreshed and ready for the day, even if you lapse on your sleep hygiene. You don't need to get everything in place. You can start putting in the groundwork tonight.

Routines heal when you create that resting space for your brain – and you can do that by turning an imperfect life into an opportunity to unfrazzle.

Exercise – A foundational routine that works for you

Think about a typical evening in.

Now think about your *foundational* evening routines. This means *activities I have to do, no matter what* or *activities I do that help me sleep*. For example, perhaps after you come in from work you have a shower, make dinner, eat dinner and prepare your stuff for the next day. That's a foundational routine. Maybe, in addition, you give your children a bath and read them a story so *they'll* go to sleep (meaning you will too).

In your notebook, under the heading **my foundational evening routine**, write only the things you *have* to do – either because they need to be done, or because they help you to sleep. Perhaps you practise yoga, because it unwinds you and helps you relax. Perhaps you watch an episode of a TV programme – if it genuinely helps you to relax and go to sleep, it's in.

Look back at your answers to the exercise *What's your evening frazzle?* to remind you of what is frazzling about your nights in. If any routine is a part of your evening frazzle, leave it out.

Foundational evening routines:

- are things you *have to do*
- are things you do because they help you sleep
- do not frazzle you

Detention stories – Khalil

Khalil is 54 years old, has had little formal education, and doesn't speak much English. We communicate anyway, as much as we can. He is one of the most peaceful people I've ever met, despite the challenges of his situation. In the morning he takes a walk around the little courtyard garden, and then does some gentle exercise in the gym. He reads the paper in the library in his own language, and then comes to the class for an hour to improve his English. After lunch he calls his family, goes to the gym again, and comes to the class again. After dinner he plays a game with his friends or watches TV. In between, he prays regularly. Over time I've seen him depleted by the difficulties of his life as it is right now, but he never varies in his routine.

'Doing the same thing every day helps my head,' he says – with his friend translating when he struggles to communicate as he wishes. 'I've got too much stress up here, but going to the gym, coming here, doing this, that, and the other – it helps me to be calm. It stops me thinking too much.'

Routines don't have to be rigid

Every decision to be made tires the brain, however slightly, and if you're frazzled – or under extreme stress like Khalil – committing to a routine takes away the pressure to have to make constant choices about how to spend your time.

That doesn't mean you must stick to it rigidly. The point of a routine is *it's there for when you need it*. It needn't prevent spontaneity. Changing the routine, switching things about to see what happens – this is great exercise for the brain, to prevent it entrenching those deeply-grooved pathways. Being detained quite suddenly – as it always is, for it never comes with a warning – is such a crazy change to a person's life, that embedding those routines as Khalil has done has been essential for him to retain a sense of peace.

If your life is relatively stable, experiment with routines. The Wind-Down Zone – which you'll read about shortly – is a guideline which you can follow as strictly or as loosely as you think is best for you. Once you understand it, and you've followed it for a bit, try adapting it for your life as it is now. Then later, maybe you'll need to adapt again.

However, resting space is *crucial* to allowing you to have a better night's sleep, and that's what you're going to do now, with your new, less-than-perfect, evening routine.

(If you work shifts, take 'evening' to mean the time at the end of your shift).

iv) The Wind-Down Zone

Routines require commitment and focus. This means that when you have the opportunity, commit yourself to an evening in with a focus on unfrazzling. Then do the same the next time another opportunity comes along.

Here is a chance to nurture yourself by taking care of your frazzle. Whether you have other people to take care of, or you arrive home late from work (or both), there's always a small opportunity to look after yourself within a chaotic space.

It might be just an hour, or it could be more; if you're able, you could choose to take it as the entire evening up until you go to bed.

The Wind-Down Zone gives the brain true downtime to process, sort and file the events of the day. This means:

- Time off from fatiguing 'brain-work.' This might mean checking emails, web-surfing, reading and replying to message group chats, and so on. Even gaming – which many people do to unwind – can be fatiguing for a brain that's been staring at a screen all day. Doing your accounts is fatiguing – it's not downtime.
- Time off from being busy. The Wind-Down Zone is slow, thoughtful, and it's step by step, not ten things at once.
- Time off from pursuing what is best, optimum, perfect, or ideal. In the Wind-Down Zone, you'll say, *that'll do*.

Exercise – Step by step to the Wind-Down Zone

1. Decide now how much time you can realistically carve out for the Wind-Down Zone (the longer, the better). This doesn't mean *after* all the chores have been done and everything's

sorted for tomorrow. It means *from* the point you decide *no more fatiguing brain-work, being busy, pursuing the best choice.* I would like everyone to begin the Wind-Down Zone from the point they come in through the door, because the more unfrazzling time you have before bed, the better you'll be able to sleep.

If you're unsure, start with one hour, and work backwards. The hard-and-fast rule is, *it must be up until the point of bedtime.* You can't have the Wind-Down Zone between 6 and 7pm, and then return to your emails and texting afterwards. It won't work to help you sleep, because you'll be filling your brain with dopamine and stress hormones, plus overworking it so it will have no time to process, sort and file those emails and texts until you fall into bed.

The Wind-Down Zone is downtime for your brain to process, sort and file in the hours before bed.

Write in your notebook when the Wind-Down Zone begins.

2. Tell people what you are doing, especially the people who are likely to message you late at night. When it comes to the Wind-Down Zone Rules, explain how and why you are doing it: giving your brain time off before bed, in order to help you sleep.

3. Go back to the smartphone-control exercises from Chapter 2: *How to beat the emotional brain* and *Pick your frazzle stop* to help when you feel that compulsion to pick up your phone. If you do pick it up by accident, go back to the *Feel-good loop* in the same chapter.

Basic Rules for the Wind-Down Zone
No fatiguing brain-work

No busyness
No pursuing the best possible choice

Exercise: How to avoid fatiguing brain-work

Write the following (or whatever activity is appropriate for you) on sticky notes and put them somewhere prominent; your phone, your laptop – anywhere you might be likely to be drawn into fatiguing frazzle.

The Wind-Down Zone [write your start time here]

1. No emails.
2. No social media.
3. No clicking through links.
4. No gaming.
[or whatever is appropriate]

Depending on how strong your compulsion to do any of the above is, put your phone in a drawer, a bag, or a room you won't go into. Do the quiz in Chapter 2 to ascertain how addicted you are to your devices. Perhaps – from the moment you come in through the door – you're able to pick your phone up to read a text, put it down and not think about it again.

Most of us can't – that's why the Wind-Down Zone must begin at *the moment you stop your fatiguing brain-work*. If you feel compelled to text throughout the evening, *every night* (and it is a compulsion, to do it every night) set a time at *least* one hour before bed, when you'll stop. That will be your the Wind-Down Zone.

If you think giving yourself one entire evening a week without a phone works better for you, do that instead. Then later maybe you'll be able to try two.

What works best for me is *no texting after 9pm* and *no other brain-work after 7pm* – except on the odd occasion when it seems absolutely necessary. I've been practising this for a long time, and it took trial and error to understand what was best for me. Because we are all different, what works for me won't be the same as what works for you.

Exercise: How to avoid busyness and the optimum choice

1. Embrace imperfection and do less stuff

At home, we're overwhelmed with choice. Hundreds of films on our streaming service, a thousand songs online, countless podcasts. Yet there is no such thing as the 'perfect choice.' We are also told constantly that we must be *achieving* and *doing stuff*, in order to be valuable human beings. This is also a nonsense. Both those ideas frazzle us.

My great-great uncle Albert died a few years ago, aged 96. He fought in World War Two, and later cared for his wife who suffered with Parkinson's disease for 15 years. He had good reason to feel stressed and frazzled. Yet he was the brightest, most chilled-out person I've ever known.

When I once asked him about how he managed to stay so relaxed, he told me, in his broad Sheffield accent:

'I used to be so particular, Stephanie. You wouldn't believe it! Oh yes... this is no good, that's no good. It's since me wife died [in 1996] you see. I decided after that, nothing was going to bother me any more. I'll have tea

with sugar or without. I'll stand up or sit down. I don't mind anything now.'

It's sometimes a struggle to accept less than perfect, and to stop always being busy. But if we can, it's good for our brain. If we can learn to be as laid-back as Great-Great Uncle Albert, we'll be very happy people.

2. Make a plan.

Decide in advance **what you will do during your evening.** In the bedtime story earlier, you chose beforehand which album to listen to and which show to watch. You don't have to create a fully-planned schedule, but decide before you start flicking through your music choices, and before you switch on the TV. As you become used to this routine, you'll find yourself listening to one podcast (for example), and mentally planning when you'll listen to the next.

Don't get lured in to flicking through hundreds of films on Netflix, for example.

3. Do things offline where possible.

You might only store music on your phone – as opposed to a laptop or tablet. I recommend downloading them, and switching to flight mode during your Wind-Down Zone, plus maybe get an app that you can set to return to connectivity when you want. You might prefer to use a tablet or laptop for media, so your phone can remain in another room.

4. If you're online, give yourself one change of mind only.

Stop flicking over and over again. Don't change your mind

halfway through and flick over. If the music / show / whatever is truly terrible, **switch it off.**

That's **two choices only: on or off.**

5. No more than one screen-based activity at a time.

If you're offline, and have committed to not websurfing, there won't be the same capacity to do more than one screen-based activity at a time. But if you're used to checking the internet while watching a TV show, it can be hard to resist having your phone or tablet nearby and picking it up under some pretext or other.

It can feel uncomfortable to remain with one screen-based activity at a time. However, if your brain is occupied with two or more screen-based activities at once, you'll feel easily fatigued and frazzled.

6. Move and speak slowly.

Slowing your movements and your speech will help to put your nervous system into **parasympathetic,** the resting state for the body and brain. (You can either be stressed *or* relaxed, not both together: if you're a tiny bit stressed, you're not in parasympathetic). This state is essential for restful sleep. Going to bed in a state of tension or hyperactivity, trying to cram in a dozen 'essential' activities before night-time, will disrupt your deep sleep pattern.

v) Common-sense tips for better sleep

Since beginning my research into Unfrazzle, I've accumulated a variety of tips and fixes to help with sleep. Combined with the Wind-Down Zone, many of them have really helped me, and I've detailed how and why each tip might work for you.

1. Not too hot, not too cold

The temperature of the bedroom can aid or disrupt our sleep. Because we're all different, you may sleep better with a warmer room or a colder room. You might need a thick-tog duvet or a lighter one, wear fleecy pyjamas or nothing. A lot of people benefit from a constant flow of fresh air through the night. Try with the window open a crack, and learn whether that helps.

The issue here is in sharing a room with a partner (or someone else) who has different temperature needs to you. Separate single duvets with different togs may help, with the bedroom kept at the coolest temperature you can both cope with.

2. Keep the room dark

Daylight sends a message to your brain to wake up. Especially in the summer months, shut out as much natural light as you can from the room by installing blackout curtains and/or blinds. You can buy stick-on blackout blinds to cut out the light from the top part of the window if daylight is still bleeding through. I used to staple bits of blackout blinds to the ceiling of the bedroom where the roller blind let in light.

You can also buy a sleep mask, which will stop light affecting your eyes. However, daylight on *any part of the body will send a 'wake-up' message to the brain.*

3. Wear amber-shaded glasses at night

So-called 'blue light' – which comes from LED lights and the light from screens – interferes with your circadian rhythm and the body's release of melatonin, disrupting your sleep patterns.

Wearing amber-shaded glasses in the evening will encourage your brain to feel sleepy. If that feels too much, then at least wear them to watch TV (or get a blue-light filter for your tech), and if you go out to a late-night supermarket, for example, (these often have bright LED lights) put them on while you stand in the queue.

4. Have a hot soothing drink before bed

Chamomile and valerian both have sleep-encouraging properties. Golden milk (turmeric, black pepper, cinnamon, milk + sweetener, whisked together and heated gently) may also help to send you off.

Ashwagandha is an ancient Ayurvedic herb, used in India for centuries as both energiser and sleep-enhancer. You can take capsules before bed, or buy powder and whisk that in to your golden milk also*.

Consult your doctor or other medical practitioner before taking any supplements for sleep.

5. Balance your blood sugar

Before I learned to balance my blood sugar I'd often be unable to fall asleep, lying awake with thoughts racing round my head. It was a revelation to realise the problem wasn't psychological, but physiological – and much easier to fix.

Fast carbs that contain sugars (white bread, pasta, rice, chips, sugary desserts and so on) must be balanced with protein and healthy fats to ensure your body isn't dumped with insulin, which will spike your blood sugar above its stable limit and can lead to that racing mind.

If you're unsure how to go about this, buy a recipe book that focuses on balancing blood sugar. You can also buy a blood sugar meter that will monitor to some extent how you're absorbing the carbs from food.

6. Meditation and breath-work

Listening to a yoga nidra (sleep yoga) recording, or other sleep-based meditation as you lie in bed may help you to drop off to sleep more deeply. But be careful of anything internet-based if it's by your bed. I recommend downloading something and listening to it on the sofa for example, so you can leave your phone there as you then stumble into bed.

You can also try breath-work to help you sleep. In Chapter Five I'll detail a body-and-breath exercise to try, which you can also use at night. Basically, deep belly breaths in, but longer belly breaths out are the key to a parasympathetic state. Keep going for ten minutes or so at night until you start to feel tired.

7. Don't stay in bed if you can't sleep

If you wake up in the night and habitually can't fall back asleep, don't stay there. Get up, go in another room, get a glass of water, go to the toilet, have a light snack (it might be your blood sugar that needs balancing). Whatever you do, **don't** pick up your phone or put on the TV – way too stimulating for your brain. Read a book, stare at the night sky, write a page full of thoughts.

8. No tech in the bed

Remove all tech from your bedroom (except an alarm clock). If you have a go-to for getting to sleep – such as reading a page from a novel, or writing a diary, keep that beside you. But the primary purpose of the bedroom is for loving and sleeping **only**. This will enable your brain to make that connection, so when you're lying in bed, you will associate it only with those two activities, and not with watching TV or checking emails. You will be much more likely to sleep.

If you work in your bedroom – as I used to – zone off an area that's not your bed for working in. A desk and a chair with your computer will suffice. As long as you don't work from bed, it shouldn't impede your sleep.

9. Get the day out of your head

Buy a notebook (another one!) and spend fifteen minutes writing whatever thoughts come into your head on to the page. If you wake in the night, you can keep it beside you open at a blank page, and scribble anything that comes to you. It might be memories, thoughts, or stuff you need to do tomorrow. It may enable you to empty your head of the clutter, and help you sleep.

10. Go to your GP

Sleeping tablets do not work to get you into that deep, restful sleep. They will only remove your conscious mind from being awake – which is a break after all, but it won't send the important bit of your brain to sleep. Sleeping tablets also lose their efficacy after only a short time. A placebo tablet may work just as well.

In the UK, you can also ask for a referral to an NHS sleep disorder clinic. There, you may be invited to sleep overnight so you can be monitored for sleep apnoea and restless leg syndrome. This, again, may help.

11. Sort your partner's sleep

Your bed-partner's sleep habits have huge potential to disrupt yours. If one can sleep, the other is more likely to as well. Ask them to put in place all the tips above, and ideally to take on the Wind-Down Zone along with you. If you're both relaxed and unfrazzled, you'll help one another to sleep better.

Chapter Three summed up

Why can't I sleep?

- The main cause of sleeplessness is stress.
- Stress can be from any source, physical or emotional.
- Stress can remain in the body from incidents from years before.
- Your usual evening routines may be frazzling you and preventing restful sleep.

How can I sleep?

Routines help you sleep when they create a resting space for the brain in order to unfrazzle.

What is the Wind-Down Zone?

It is your evening routine, in the time before bed without:

- Fatiguing brain-work (phones / texting / websurfing / group chats etc).
- Busyness (rushing around trying to do everything at once).
- Pursuit of the best possible choice (you don't need the perfect evening in order to unfrazzle – the opposite is actually true).

One essential quick-fix to enable your sleep:

Replace your phone with an alarm clock by the bed.

Also:

Try the other tips for sleep to see if they help with getting a decent night's rest.

In a nutshell:

If you want a better night's sleep, remove all frazzle at least one hour before bed.

CHAPTER FOUR

EVERYDAY UNFRAZZLE: HOW TO GET SPACE FOR YOURSELF

In Chapter One, you learned the basics of Unfrazzle.

In Chapter Two, you learned how to stop phones from frazzling your brain.

In Chapter Three, you began the first stage of Unfrazzle, by creating an hour or so before bed free from busyness, pursuit of 'the best', and fatiguing brain-work.

Now, in Chapter Four, you'll learn how to keep your calm topped up throughout the day, and you'll do this by embedding regular Unfrazzle into your everyday life. This means time for yourself **every day,** when your brain is not fully occupied or entertained, and you'll achieve that via what I call blank time.

Blank time gives you a thrice-daily Mini-Unfrazzle of ten minutes each. That's thirty minutes a day – or longer if you're able – to give your nervous system and brain some time off from all the hard work they do. You'll learn how and why the human race has put a halt to blank time, how most of us have colluded in that, and why lack of it has led to the new age of frazzle.

You'll be walked step by step towards inputting blank time into your everyday life. This, plus The Wind-Down Zone from Chapter Three, plus the tricks you learned in Chapter Two to leave your phone alone, is crucial to recovering that sense of freedom you used to have; a freedom that *I know* is 100% possible for you to get back.

In addition, maybe you have the space, ability – and, in some cases, the funds – to get some really deep blank time, in order to let your nervous system unwind. If you find yourself committed to the regularity of blank time, and want to achieve yet more, I'll end with a list of tips for things you can do to totally sink into that Unfrazzle.

However, *Unfrazzle* is about the routine, not the one-off. It's every day, not every year or even every month. That's why, by the end of this chapter, you'll not only be giving yourself permission to give your brain time out throughout the day, you'll see that although time to unfrazzle may seem a luxury, it's not. Its potential is in your life as you already live it – and it's about turning the everyday grind into an opportunity to unwind.

i) Everyday grind

Quiz – what's your everyday grind?

Imagine that today is just an ordinary day. There is no emergency and no holiday; it's not even Sunday. Today contains stuff that we have to do. Things that annoy us, or nag at us, or are just a bit *meh*.

Answer the questions to discover your particular everyday grind.

1. It's a cold winter's morning. The alarm goes. How do you feel?
   a) Fine, if you can spend time on your phone before the day becomes inevitable.
   b) Exhausted. You drag yourself from the covers, cursing.
   c) Energised. You leap up and go for a brisk jog.

2. Time for breakfast. What's your routine?
   a) What's breakfast?
   b) Put the kettle on, call the kids, get breakfast together, search for your keys, look at the clock, check the bus times, search for your bag … etc etc.
   c) Eat your homemade granola while listening to Radio 3.

3. You're travelling by bus or train, or sitting in a car. What do you do?
   a) Use your phone or laptop.
   b) Read a book or the paper.
   c) Nothing.

4. It's lunchtime. What do you do?

a) What's lunchtime?

b) Eat your lunch while using your phone, reading a book, or making calls.

c) Eat lunch.

5. You're walking home. What do you do?

a) Put your head down and speed up to get it over with.

b) Return that phone call, listen to that podcast, type that text.

c) Move slowly, despite the hurlyburly around you.

6. Time for housework. How do you approach it?

a) Minimally. They're called chores for a reason.

b) Maximally. You start one chore, halfway through check your phone, get distracted by something more interesting, then you look up and the house is in a worse mess than before you started.

c) Mindfully. You choose one chore, and do it carefully, without any other distractions.

7. The plants are looking thirsty. What are your thoughts?

a) They're supposed to be brown, aren't they?

b) Kill them with your overzealousness.

c) Water them slowly, even if it takes forever.

8. The kitchen's in a mess. What do you do?

a) Close the door.

b) Tidy it in a rush to get on with the other hundred things you need to do.

c) Tidy it with love.

9. It's time for the weekly food shop. How do you approach it?

a) Order it all online while you're watching TV.

b) Dash around the supermarket throwing things into your basket, checking the time because you have to be somewhere else like, thirty minutes ago.

c) You enjoy it. What could be better than getting food in for the family?

10. You have an appointment in half an hour at a place you've never been to. It's ten minutes' walk away. What's more likely for you?

a) You keep forgetting what it is, where it is, and when it is. You have to keep checking the details on your phone.

b) You plan to leave exactly ten minutes before, because you can't bear being early, and there's loads you can get done before you have to leave.

c) You get ready and leave the house, taking your time to walk there and knowing if you're early it doesn't matter.

Answers

Mostly As

Daily life is a grind, isn't it? You'd rather it were Friday night, that moment when you walk into the pub or restaurant, and your friends cheer your arrival, with the entire weekend to come. The best way through the week is to put your head down and get on with it, while looking forward to fun.

Mostly Bs

Life isn't so much a grind, as a never-ending, mammoth list of stuff to do. Sometimes you feel your head's about to fall off with the pressure, and you're on your own with it all, and nobody's lending a hand. You dream of a beach in Thailand, or a hilltop town in Tuscany, a leisurely coffee beside you, a novel in your hand and sunshine on your head.

Mostly Cs

You're able to embrace, to some extent, the everyday grind. Now look again at where you chose any As or Bs – here is where your focus begins. (And if you didn't choose any As or Bs then you're amazing – or perhaps deluded.)

My everyday grind

The alarm clock hauls me out of bed at half past six. In the winter, it's dark as I leave the house, huddled against the cold as I walk down the hill to the station, where I stand on the platform with hundreds of other commuters awaiting the 07:46 train. We squash on to seats, fingers crossed for no delays, and when I arrive at my station I squeeze out of the carriage and go up into one of the busiest airports in the country.

It's crammed with holidaymakers and their luggage, chain stores, neon lighting and flickering overhead signs. I walk through Arrivals, weaving between people emerging from the automatic doors, and the lines of people waiting to greet them. I go down the steps at the other end and out into the concrete guts of the airport, the part that the passengers don't see.

I walk past the buildings that contain the staff who support the running of the airport, towards the bus stop in front of the aircrew offices. There, I await a bus that will take me along a busy main road, turning off into one of the perimeter roads that span the airport, and eventually drop me near the detention centre where I work.

At the end of the day, of course, I do the same thing in reverse.

I've had this commute for almost twenty years, as the number of travellers passing through the airport – and the number of commuters – have expanded exponentially. There are more stores crammed into the same space, more infoscreens, and video advertisements where there used to be a single paper banner.

Commuting frazzles. A 2014 study by the Office for National Statistics found that commuters have lower life satisfaction, lower levels of happiness and higher anxiety, the worst being for journeys between 60 and 90 minutes. I used to cope by putting my head down and getting on with it. Like most of my fellow commuters, I distracted myself where possible, escaping into a book or my phone.

Yet out of this situation – a situation that enabled me to live in the city of my choice and have a job that I loved – I learned to unfrazzle. Commuting was one of my daily challenges to calm – it still is – and seeing it as an opportunity, rather than an endurance test, enabled me to start reframing the experience.

The opportunity expanded into other areas. If I'd answered the everyday grind quiz a few years ago, my answers would have been mostly As or Bs. My everyday life was – and still is – full of stuff I needed to do. In those days, however, I saw it as something to be endured. I either rushed through chores and obligations, or if I had any so-called 'nothing' time I used it to achieve stuff on my to-do list. For example, if I was waiting in the supermarket queue I'd use the time to check my emails. If I had ten minutes before I had to leave the house I would cram it full of fifteen minutes' worth of stuff.

I haven't got rid of that desire to pack everything in. I'm only human. That's why reframing the ten minutes' wait as an opportunity to unfrazzle, rather than as a chance to do more stuff, became vital. It enabled me to embrace the '*meh*' stuff of life. Not crises, but everyday routines, and the waiting time in between those routines. Now, the 'meh' is my chance to unfrazzle a little bit further.

It's taken over my walking time, and I've discovered the potential for Unfrazzle within that. It's recalibrated the way I do everyday chores. It's helped me to adhere to the two principles of Unfrazzle – embrace imperfection, and do less stuff. Plus, adhering to those two principles helps me with sticking to the possibilities offered by the everyday grind.

These possibilities are the focus of Chapters Four and Five. In the next part of this chapter, you'll learn what blank time is, why it's necessary for Unfrazzle, and how you can get it into your everyday life.

ii) Blank time

*"There are certain half-dreaming moods of mind in
which we naturally steal away from noise and glare, and
seek some quiet haunt where we may indulge our reveries
and build our air castles undisturbed."*

Washington Irving, The Legend of Sleepy Hollow & Other Stories

In 2001, neurologist Marcus Raichle discovered that a network
of separate areas of the brain connect when we daydream.
It's a mind-wandering state that only activates while we're
not focused on a particular task, when we are more relaxed,
when our brain 'cuts loose.' He named it the *default mode* of
the brain, because he found that our brain always returns to
that state after it has finished focusing.

His discovery found that the part of the brain involved
during this time is a hive of activity. It also uses a different
metabolism to the rest of the brain, and because of the parts
of the brain that are used, has huge implications for our
health and wellbeing. It involves, amongst other areas, the
prefrontal cortex (which controls our 'clever brain') and the
hippocampus (where our memories are stored). These are
the areas that are attacked by Alzheimer's disease: they are
the brain areas that make us who we are.

The mind-wandering state can be challenging for people
suffering anxiety, because it allows space for unhelpful,
repetitive thoughts. I've experienced that myself, and that's
why I've adapted it for Unfrazzle using a process I call 'blank
time.'

Blank time activates the default mode, but it does more than that. Blank time is truly healing and unfrazzling, and it can be accessed from within your everyday routines. That's the so-called daily grind; not the high drama, but the dull, obligatory nitty-gritty, and it has the potential to give you back headspace and calm.

The difference between the default mode and blank time

The default mode, or mind-wandering network, is activated any time the brain is not focused on a specific task. For example, lying still in bed with your eyes closed would activate the default mode.

However, blank time goes further, by occupying the brain in a very minor way. Combining the default mode with this slight activity is a direct way into Unfrazzle. It will help you to feel calm, it will give you a sense of perspective, and it will enable you to come up with creative ideas and solutions to problems, much more effectively than you'd get from simply lying down and closing your eyes.

If you're frazzled, you might already have a potential go-to activity – or two, or three – that brings your brain down from stress, that resets you, and makes you better able to thrive. This can be some form of exercise or hobby. However, that unfrazzling activity is often an extra that you incorporate into your day: a morning run, evening yoga – rather than something you absolutely *have* to do. That's great, but this plan is all about not asking you to add an extra. So keep anything that helps with Unfrazzle, but the potential of blank time lies in incorporating it into the nitty-gritty routines of everyday life.

The two main features of blank time

No external, specific task to focus on (so enabling the mind-wandering network)

The brain enables the mind-wandering network, or default mode, when there is no external focus. If you're in conversation, or reading a book, or examining a painting, your brain is focused on something outside of itself. When your mind drifts from topic to topic within itself, it is mind-wandering.

Keeping the body/brain occupied in a minor way (the extra that makes it blank time)

This can be, for example, walking, moving the hands, or when we observe exterior movement, but do not focus on one thing in particular – gazing out of the window at trees bending in the breeze, for example. Even when I was floored with difficult emotions, that slight activity helped to release my brain from unhelpful thought patterns. (And by the way, in Chapter Five you'll learn how to *really* tackle those thought-loops and regain your true calm – so hang in there).

Exercise: What is blank time?

Think now about what moments or activities in regular life might constitute blank time. It might be something you already do, or something that occurs to you now. Have a look at the list below if you need any prompting.

- Gazing out of a train window at nothing in particular.
- Doing daily housework.

- Walking in the countryside.
- Standing in the shower (sensation of water on skin occupies the body).
- 'Mindless' gardening (as opposed to concentrating on a task).
- Gentle exercise.
- Colouring in.
- Cooking a meal you know well.

Try to think of three things.

Remember, it must be when you **don't need to focus on a particular task.** It's when you're doing something so familiar your mind can wander, when your body's relaxed. Specifically, it's when your brain is not working to process external stimuli. And it must involve **the body or brain being occupied in a minor way.**

In some of these activities, you'll switch in and out of the mind-wandering network. So when you cook a meal you know well, you have to find the ingredients (concentrate), and then cook (mind-wandering). Because it's default, your mind will automatically return to mind-wandering when it's given the opportunity. It can't be forced there. This is part of the potential of blank time as an everyday Unfrazzle.

About flow

Flow is characterised as when you are fully immersed in the activity you are doing, and when you feel as if you *are* the activity. Some of the activities in the list above can involve flow, if the moment is right – gardening, cooking a meal you know well, maybe exercise too.

However, blank time is not necessarily flow – because flow is like a wave: you can catch it, or you can miss it. Doing an activity but missing the flow can feel frustrating. Blank time is much easier to access than that.

Flow also often involves total concentration – which is not blank time – and it often requires you to add the activity into your day. An intense exercise class can put you in a flow state, when you are completely in your body, and can be a great way to unfrazzle. Blank time, however, is different: it's already part of your day-to-day life, and the only effort it requires is that you resist the urge to get rid of it.

Because the one problem with blank time is that we will sometimes do almost anything not to be in it, even though it's the way our brain wants to be. Over the years, we've eradicated it from our lives until we're where we are now, the era of zero blank time.

iii) How we got rid of blank time (but it wasn't our fault)

The need for blank time is a modern phenomenon, because in the pre-digital age, we had it much more often. Even if we distracted ourselves from empty, nothing-y time with books or newspapers, music or TV, there were still minutes – hours, even – in our day with nothing to do but let our mind drift and wander. As a child, Sundays seemed endless: no shops open, nothing on the telly. It was a day filled with blank time opportunities, although I didn't think that way then.

As the digital age has progressed, the human race has become used to eradicating blank time from our lives. We fill the empty moments of our day with flicking through our phones, with checking out websites, with constant busyness, with pursuing 'the best.'

I used to be the same. Eventually I realised that all that activity wasn't doing me any favours, but then something worse happened: I started blaming myself for my behaviour.

I thought it was my fault for being unable to put down my phone, for eradicating empty moments, for fearing boredom. Then I learned more about the brain and stress, and I realised it wasn't my, or any one individual's, fault. We live in a system that has created a monster, and it's in control of us, rather than the other way round.

As I wrote in Chapter One, our brains have become wired to seek frazzle. Part of that wiring means that humans have got rid of blank time from our everyday life. Below are three reasons as to why that happens.

a) Stress hormones are both uncomfortable and addictive

The stress hormones – cortisol and adrenaline – can cause us extreme discomfort: anxiety, dread, a clenched stomach, a sense of being 'frozen'.

In addition, ironically – or perhaps consequentially – we can also be addicted to stress. Stress hormones make our heart race, our breathing shorter, our senses are heightened: it's exhilarating. When people face physical extremes, they later report that they never felt so alive as when they were hanging off the end of a mountain or battling the ocean. Adrenaline doesn't care whether you're rock climbing or running for your train; it's neutral to the reason *why* it's being generated, and it will give you the same feeling either way.

Therefore, stress hormones give you two reasons to eradicate blank time.

Firstly, they can make anyone feel very uncomfortable, and so you might mask the negative sensations by distraction. It is why, in Chapter Two, you learned the value of the frazzle stop when you long to pick up your phone. Reaching for a magazine rather than your tech is like a nicotine patch for a smoker: basically, it's nowhere near as damaging as the rabbit hole of the internet, but it's not blank time.

Secondly, if you're addicted to the exhilaration of stress, you'll keep ourselves in a high-tension state – pursuing frazzle – and thereby ridding your life of blank time.

I created a life around addiction to stress hormones, and distraction from the emotions they generated. I'm *still* not over that, and perhaps I never will be. It's why I need Unfrazzle to save my life.

b) We're drawn to dopamine

As I wrote in Chapter Two, the human brain is wired to want dopamine. There's no dopamine to be found in blank time. No lists to tick, no tasks to complete, no motivation for a hit of pleasure. Why would anyone voluntarily get rid of those fun activities for a spate of what we might consider boredom instead?

Nowadays, you can pursue dopamine to the nth degree. In 2017 Sean Parker, one of the founders of Facebook, spoke of how the company had exploited our "vulnerability in human psychology" by giving its users dopamine hits. "God knows what it's doing to our children's brains," he added.[4]

Even if you don't use social media, the modern world enables you to pursue dopamine in a thousand other ways. Previously, your choice was limited. Now, it's endless.

c) Guilt about time off

Blank time is when you're not focused on an external task. To other people, it may look as if you're not doing much at all. I'm a writer, but my ideas often come when I'm not writing. I might look to other people as if I'm staring at the ceiling, but in reality my brain's working hard (honestly, it is).

Yet until the entire world realises that blank time is an essential way to unfrazzle, any of us might feel guilty at not appearing to do 'proper' work. It's like the old T-shirt slogan *Look busy, the boss is coming.* Some of us – me included – have the sensation that as long as we're doing *something,* even if it's a nonsense, we're being useful.

4   https://www.theguardian.com/technology/2017/nov/09/facebook-sean-park-er-vulnerability-brain-psychology

Yet productivity increases the more breaks we give our brain from externally-focused work, as studies have shown.[5] In any case, blank time is not 'time off' as such, because the brain is very active in the default mode. It just doesn't feel like it.

Self-test: The honesty box

This is an opportunity for you to be 100% honest with yourself, without guilt, blame or shame. No judgement here: because of the way the brain is wired, every human on the planet reaches for distraction and eliminates blank time when it's available. The only difference between us and a nomadic hunter-gatherer tribe in that respect, is that we have the opportunity.

1. Think about the last time you reached for a distraction.

- When was that?
- What did you do?
- How often do you reach for distractions?

2. Think about the last time you didn't leave yourself enough time to do something.

- What was the situation?
- How did it make you feel?
- Would you behave differently next time?

3. Think about the last time you had a ten-minute waiting period.

---

5   https://news.illinois.edu/view/6367/205427

- What did you do during those ten minutes?
- Is this part of your regular behaviour, or a one-off?

4. Think about when you last picked up your phone/other internet-wired device.

- What was the reason for that?
- What else were you doing while you did that?

5. Think about the last time you felt you had too much going on in your life (this is very possibly right now).

- How does/did that make you feel?
- Is there anything you do/did that could be dropped without any great drama, yet you resist doing so?

Remember: It really isn't our fault

I don't think it's helpful or useful to blame ourselves for being born into a world that has erased opportunities for Unfrazzle. Blank time is often free, and easily available. But we live in a world that often only sees the benefits in something which has economic value. Blank time can't be sold – or rather, it doesn't have to be. There are plenty of ways in which you can spend money to achieve it – but you don't have to.

Because blank time within our routines is not a money-spinner – if it's already there, how can it be? – every opportunity for it has been replaced with an opportunity for someone, somewhere, to make a profit. Any moment your mind can drift, and your brain enters the mind-wandering network, it is snapped back to the concrete, tangible world by a demand on your attention.

It's why my walk through the airport has transformed over twenty years from one single paper advertisement to flashing screens everywhere selling products and services.

Not only that, but if you live in a busy city – for all its energy and all its benefits, of which there are many – blank time is additionally hard to come by: cities are just so stimulating.

However, although the eradication of blank time wasn't our fault, we now have a choice. We're free. We can begin incorporating it into our lives, to get ourselves to start unfrazzling every day. Because the benefits of blank time are amazing and transformative. It could quite literally change your life.

iv) What blank time will do for you

Detention stories – Hossain

Life in detention alters the workings of the brain. Hossain is 44 years old, a natural entrepreneur who resists the means by which the immigration system and detention eliminates the humanity from people. "I am a human first, and a detainee second," is one of his favourite phrases. He has been here five months, and although he was cheerful at first, he is being crushed daily by the knockbacks he faces. Although he has retained his kind nature, and is one of the guys the officers introduce the new people to, because he reaches out the hand of friendship wherever possible, I have seen his brain malfunctioning to a large extent. I see him at two o'clock in the afternoon, on his way out of his room. "I just have to make a quick phone call, and then I'll come by," he says. He never turns up, because half way through his phone call he forgets what it is he's supposed to be doing. He comes into the class and says, "I've decided that I need to learn …." Then he appears to drift into a sort of daze. Ten minutes later he says he has to do something and will come back in a minute.

He is still intelligent and open-minded. His core character has not changed. But his brain is severely malfunctioning. It will regain its faculties once he is out of detention and in a less stressful place. But right now I see day by day how simple decisions are beyond him, how he quite simply cannot remember one thing after another. He does not have Alzheimer's or a deteriorating brain problem. He is just severely stressed.

Mini-quiz: What do you need blank time for?

1. Have you made a snap decision you've later regretted?

2. Have you ever felt overwhelmed with the need to make a decision or a choice, whether it's about something crucial or trivial?

3. Have you ever found it difficult to prioritise what needs to be done first?

4. Have you ever looked back and wondered why on earth you took such a strange course of action?

5. Have you ever lost perspective on what was important and what wasn't?

If you answered 'yes' to any of these questions, blank time will help you to **make decisions, get perspective and sort your priorities.**

Neuroscience labels the brain's problems with making decisions *choice overload or decision fatigue,* which stems from overworking the 'clever brain' (controlled by the prefrontal cortex). As we've seen, frazzle means we can feel overwhelmed with the amount of choices and decisions we have to make.

Like any machine, when the clever brain is overworked, it malfunctions. It plumps for any random choice without being able to think things through. It puts all our priorities in equal place, because it's unable to differentiate what is more important. It can't work out what is the pressing, vital issue of the day, and what can be left for another time.

My overwhelmed brain

Two years into the crisis – with so many punch-the-air highs and drastic setbacks along the way that our lives could have been a Hollywood film, I found myself in my darkest hour. This was after I'd started on my health and wellness journey, but before I'd learned to embrace imperfection and do less stuff. At precisely that time, it seemed like an excellent idea to also move to a new town, and start a new life.

I was super-stressed, overwhelmed with frazzle and on the verge of a nervous breakdown. My brain was malfunctioning – not as badly as Hossain's above, but enough that I understand viscerally how it feels to have an overwhelmed brain. I'd had previous times in my life when frazzle had led me to making snap decisions and losing perspective, but this was extreme.

How I lost perspective: I became convinced I had to keep going into work, because I thought the structure of the daily routine was really important. It was a GP who saw reality and signed me off sick with stress for the second time in two years.

How I was unable to sort my priorities: With one week until we moved house (itself a questionable priority), I was spending hours going through and 'sorting' memorabilia from my past life, instead of packing up all my belongings in readiness for the move. Three days before the move date, I semi-saw the light and made a crisis call to my family, who dropped everything to come and help.

How I was unable to make decisions: I remember standing, frozen, in my local shop, completely unable to choose between two different types of olives – and somehow being convinced that olives were essential. I would have argued the point with anyone, even my future self who told me I'd one day think myself crazy.

How blank time will benefit your brain

Basic benefits

Blank time gives your brain a break. It clears the slate, and gives you room to come to clear decisions, to order your priorities, and to solve problems.

A constantly-stimulated brain runs on dopamine and stress, and this knocks out the workings of the prefrontal cortex. Decisions, priorities, and problem-solving are all processed there, so you need your prefrontal cortex to be working well, or you'll blunder into action without being able to think things through.

Also, when you rest from frazzling stimuli, you stop depleting your brain-fuel reserves of oxygenated glucose. Resting enables your brain to build up more fuel reserves. You will feel calmer and less frazzled.

Blank time means your brain can see things with a wider perspective. You cannot make decisions unless you are in the mind-wandering mode. You need a *lot* of mind-wandering: much more than you think. Otherwise, your brain will plump for the first mode of action that appears – the snap decision.

Regular, daily inputs of blank time enable the brain to process information and put things in their place.

Greater benefits

The mind-wandering mode is where your brain attends to problems, comes up with great ideas, and does your creative thinking. It's working even while you're not aware of it. The brain is awake while your conscious mind appears asleep.

It can solve your problems without you consciously trying: sometimes when you're actually asleep, sometimes when you're daydreaming, or idly letting your thoughts drift from topic to topic.

Blank time enables you to process stimuli. As your brain processes, it solves problems, creates random connections, and comes up with ideas.

Novelist Laura Wilkinson on how blank time unfrazzled her brain and gave her the inspiration for the perfect ending.

With a deadline thirty-six hours away, in the region of 20,000 words to write and no notion of how to end the novel, I was utterly beside myself. I'd consumed copious amounts of Merlot, not slept in twenty-four hours and had exhausted my usual plot-unravelling tricks.

I went to bed and slept for six hours. On waking, I headed for my local swimming pool. It was early and the place was near-enough deserted: an older woman paddled up and down the slow lane. I joined her, focusing on the action (a leisurely breast stroke), the dazzling blue of the water, the nostril-skin-scorching smell of chlorine, and as I pootled up and down, my mind wandered. I thought about what I might have for dinner, my kids, whether or not to buy a dress I'd seen and liked in Top Shop. Everything and, crucially, nothing. What I didn't think about was the book.

Lo and behold, as I hauled myself from the water, I noticed my wedding ring. A ring. That was the key to the novel's end. I prefer swimming in the sea, but for unfrazzling, swimming lengths works wonders.

Exercise: Your genius ideas

Think back over your life. You might not, like Laura, be a novelist wrestling with a plot idea, but we've all had knotty problems to solve. Think of a moment when you came up with an idea or a plan that changed something in your life for the better.

It doesn't have to be life-transforming. It might have been small or large, but it changed things in some way. Sometimes, even small decisions can be life-changing in retrospect.

It might relate to work, to your house, to your family, to your friends.

What was the problem? Was there a relationship issue, a practical difficulty, a work-related problem?

What was the solution, and how did you solve it?

Even if there were unforeseen consequences, in the fullness of time, do you feel satisfied with how the issue was resolved?

Go back to that moment now when you came up with the idea: the 'lightbulb' or 'eureka' moment. Remember how you felt when the bits that were all up in the air settled in your mind – that moment of lightness and relief.

Once you've thought of one, you may be able to think of more, both small and large. As you go through your day today, and tomorrow, remember any that come to you. Enjoy the positive associations. Even a potentially traumatic decision – such as one to leave your partner or your job, can be ultimately satisfying if you realise it was the right thing to do.

v) Your new blank time routines

How to do the routines

The basics

There are three blank time routines: *Public Transport, The Calmest Walk* and *Everyday Tasks.*

The aim is to get thirty minutes minimum of blank time per day: ten minutes each one.

If you can get one of each routine then that will give you some variety. If you don't take public transport regularly, then do one calmest walk, and two everyday tasks, for example.

If you don't regularly walk by yourself anywhere either, then you can do thirty minutes of *Everyday Tasks* instead. However, variety helps with Unfrazzle, so if possible, think about where else you can plug in some blank time that's not listed here.

If you're able to enter blank time for longer, each extra minute will unfrazzle you. But better to start small and build, than do too much and not be able to keep it up.

What you need to know

The blank time routines here are **not** an extra, unless you want them to be. They can be incorporated into your already-existing everyday life.

The aim of the activities is to **use your routines as opportunities to unfrazzle.**

They are super simple, but at the same time they'll sometimes be difficult to achieve. Why? Because, like me, you're a fellow human, and so you might:

- distract yourself from blank time, because blank time allows the brain space for uncomfortable emotions.

- pursue frazzle, because stress can feel exhilarating.
- desire dopamine, which you cannot get during blank time.
- feel guilty about doing 'nothing'.

However, blank time works. Inputting it has transformed my Unfrazzle. So if you find the routines difficult, remember the following:

- stress hormones need to be processed from the body, and blank time enables this.
- stress is exhilarating, but it is also very damaging.
- too much dopamine is damaging to the brain.
- doing 'nothing' is not an indulgence. It is a necessity.

The more you plug blank time into your regular, everyday life, the more it will become a part of your routine, and the less you'll seek distraction, frazzle and stress. This is because your brain is plastic, and the more a behaviour is reinforced, and the less another one is activated, the stronger the routine becomes.

It can take up to three months to transform a routine into an automatic behaviour, so have patience.

Public transport is an opportunity

Commuting by public transport gives me a golden opportunity to escape into blank time. The train journey between my home station and the airport is half an hour. During that time, my brain has the chance to sift through problems, issues, the events of the day. There is something about sitting by the window, looking at the shifting scenery and the lack of distinct focus that really plugs me into the mind-wandering mode, much more than sitting staring out at a static view will do.

However, I rarely get a window seat. Sometimes the carriage is so crowded I have to stand. Yet even if there's no view, I close or lower my eyes and for at least ten minutes of that journey, escape into blank time.

I also take the bus when I travel to the next town. There, too, I take the chance to engage with blank time for at least ten minutes of each journey. If there's a text I need to send, I aim to do it after the ten minutes have passed (I say *aim*. Being human, I don't always succeed – although most of the time, I do). When I'm in London travelling by tube, I don't close my eyes, but I let my gaze rest on the ground, or in my lap, for some quality blank time in the bowels of the city.

Exercise: Public transport blank time

Follow the instructions step by step in order to create a ten-minute time out for your brain.

If you travel with a companion, tell them you're switching off for ten minutes. They might relish the prospect of a short period alone themselves.

1. If you're easily distracted by conversation, plug yourself into a noise-cancelling track or background music (for more information on this, see the *Create an Unfrazzle bubble* exercise).

2. If you know you'll be tempted by your phone, put it on flight mode or put it on silent.

3. If you're in a window seat, stare out of the window at the passing scenery. Try to let your eyes blur. If there is still too much information to take in, stare upwards at the sky or the ceiling of the platforms.

4. If it's dark outside, or you're not beside a window, either look down at your lap or your feet, or, if you feel safe to do so, close your eyes (again, see *Create an Unfrazzle bubble* to create a barrier between you and the world).

5. Don't try to control your thoughts, as tricky as that might feel.

6. Tell yourself that after ten minutes, you can return to your phone/book/game/whatever.

7. If you travel regularly, increase your blank time by a minute per day.

Recommendations

- Go for blank time at the start, rather than the end of your journey, as you're more likely to do it.
- If you're worried about missing your stop, set the timer on your phone to go off at the right time.
- If you can only manage one minute, rather than ten, no problem, it's a start. We are all a work in progress.

If you don't travel by public transport regularly, then do this whenever you take a journey by bus, train or coach. Double up on the *Walking blank time exercise* instead.

On being driven by car

At the age of 21 and working for the summer in San Francisco, two Irish guys and I decided to take a mammoth 4-day road trip across the south-western bit of the States.

It turns out that America is quite a bit bigger to drive through than the UK, and in addition it also transpired that the two

Irish guys hadn't yet learned to drive. Luckily, at the eleventh hour we found an Australian guy who was travelling across the States, and he agreed to share the driving with me.

Driving for eight hours down a single-lane highway was more fun than it sounds on paper (although perhaps that's the effect of being 21), but what beat it all was when the Australian took his turn to drive. I sat in the passenger seat and gazed out at the big skies of the desert for hours, nobody in the car speaking, all of us lost in our own thoughts. It was blank time *par excellence*, at a time when frazzle was a concept more alien to me than the cactus-studded landscape we were driving through. It inspired me so much that even though being driven down a British motorway can't quite rival the romance of a desert highway in Arizona, I still find much to relish if I'm ever offered the opportunity.

If you're given the chance of being driven somewhere, without feeling obliged to provide conversation / directions / snacks, then take it as a chance to get in some really deep blank time – as long as your kindly driver and fellow passengers allow it, of course. Tell them you're switching off for ten minutes in order to recharge your batteries. They may get used to the idea very quickly, and accept it as totally normal.

As you switch off, follow the step-by-step instructions for the public transport exercise.

A walk to save your life

Those of us fortunate enough to be able to walk in our everyday life don't often appreciate its benefits. It is incredible exercise, rids our body of toxins, clears our mind, and frees us from frazzle.

However, we also often live in hectic urban environments. For thirteen years I lived in a flat on a main road, and from early in the morning until late at night there was a never-ending rumble of traffic going past the window. City life is exciting and cosmopolitan, and offers huge benefits, but it's hard to walk anywhere in a city without encountering cars, bicycle couriers, challenging fellow citizens, grabs on our attention and other barriers to calm and peace.

Yet despite the challenges, a daily walk is an opportunity to input blank time. I started my blank time walks while living in that main road flat, and I continue the same routine today. At the weekend, I often get up early and before I have my breakfast I leave the house and head for my nearest green space.

I also do this when I'm away from home. Even if there is no green space, an early-morning walk along a quiet street is adequate blank time to unfrazzle.

However, that's an extra, not an integral part of my routine, which is why it's easier to drop and harder to do. Now, whether I'm walking to the supermarket at the weekend, or going to and from the station on my way to work, I take the longer, quieter route when possible. It's already a part of my routine, which means I can input blank time with only a very little effort, and give my brain a chance to unfrazzle.

Exercise: Walking blank time

1. Think of the places you walk to regularly, and write them in your notebook. Ideally, you'll be on your own as you walk, or able to tell the person you're with that you need a little zone-out en route. If you usually drive, consider whether walking could be an option, for at least part of the journey.

You might walk to:

- the shops
- school to pick up children
- college or workplace
- an exercise class
- the station
- the house of a friend or family

… plus of course you'll walk home, when doing the journey in reverse.

2. Plan a 'calmest route' for that walk, that will take you at least ten minutes to walk from start to finish:

- Choose a quieter parallel route to the quicker, yet more hectic one – via back streets rather than a main road.
- Go via a park or other green space if you can.
- You might also choose to go earlier, if that's a quieter time, or later if that will give you a calmer route.

3. Put your phone onto flight mode, silent or leave it behind.

4. If the route is still too hectic for you to enter blank time, and you feel safe to do so, use the tools in *Create an Unfrazzle bubble* to block out part of the world.

5. As you walk, let go of any conscious thinking. *There is nothing you have to do*. You don't have to consciously work through a problem that's bothering you. The exercise alone enables your brain to wander.

Recommendations

- If this exercise is totally new for you, start with one walk, once a week and build up slowly.
- If you drive, park the car a ten-minute walk away from your destination, at least once a week. This will start to give you a bit of blank time. Blank time is *mind-wandering plus movement*, and so driving is a challenge to this. You might consider those ten minutes to be time you can't afford to plug in (I totally get that), and if that's so then focus on other regular walking you already do instead.
- If you walk a dog every day, you may already do a version of walking blank time. However, some dogs require more attention than others, and therefore can pull you out of blank time before your ten minutes is up. If that walk isn't enough for you to unfrazzle, focus on your non-dog walks – where you need to take responsibility for nothing but yourself – and see if it's possible to get yet more Unfrazzle into your life.

Everyday tasks to unfrazzle

Everyday tasks are so-called chores; things we all have to do on a daily basis. Whatever age or gender we are, however rich or poor, none of us can escape everyday tasks.

Like most of us, I have a tendency to groan when faced with a mountain of washing up. I've had that sinking feeling on coming across mulch at the bottom of the fridge, or the growing accumulation of living room mess. I'm not Julie Andrews in *The Sound of Music* or *Mary Poppins*, relentlessly cheerful in the face of adversity. I'm only human.

However I've found that seeing the cleaning out of the vegetable drawer as an opportunity to unfrazzle helps me to keep my mind on track, and also dampens down that sense that there's something else I'd rather be doing.

I also love listening to the radio when doing some mind-numbing everyday task. However, I also input ten minutes minimum of blank time as I do it – whichever task it happens to accompany. I get to listen to my podcasts, and have blank time – win-win.

As time's gone on this behaviour's become automatic. I don't think that sinking feeling will ever go, but at least I can see there's a double benefit to the never-ending nature of everyday tasks.

How everyday tasks offer us an opportunity to unfrazzle

They involve movement.

Just as with walking or travelling, 'mindless' movement enables our minds to wander.

They enable 'autopilot'

If a chore is done in the same way, repeatedly, it becomes repetitive and easy. Our brain doesn't have to work hard or pay attention. Part of our mind is occupied on doing the task, but the mind-wandering mode is free to go where it will.

The task itself is closed

There is something pleasing to the brain in achieving a simple closed task. The daily round is never-ending, but the task itself ends – washing the dishes, weeding the garden, cleaning tools.

Jasmine unfrazzles by doing a daily spiritual practice. She's a single mum with a demanding job, and below is her take on never-ending everyday chores.
I call housework 'the new computer game' because it gives you a happy feeling. You know, you have a task and then when you do it, it feels good. But it's also never over, just like a computer game. So I think why not call it that, instead?
Seeing as I have to do so much housework – plus looking after a three-year-old child means I'm constantly 'on', I think I might as well make a virtue of it, and then look at my lovely clean kitchen and enjoy it for all of five minutes before my daughter spills her food everywhere!

Exercise: Everyday tasks blank time

1. Choose *one* blank time everyday task. It must be:

- A task you do on a regular basis.
- Easy, mindless and autopilot-enabling.
- Involving some movement with the hands or body.
- Of a ten-minute duration or longer (the longer the better).

Look at the table for examples of what is and is not a blank time chore. Choose one of these, or one from your own list, or something completely different.

Blank time tasks	Brain-work tasks
Cooking an easy meal you know well	Cooking a meal from a new recipe

Washing up	Checking bank statements
Painting a wall	Painting something small and intricate
Weeding the garden	Planning your new garden
Vacuuming	A chore done irregularly that involves some element of re-learning throughout (putting together shelving units, perhaps)
Washing the car	Any chore involving decision-making (hanging up the washing, sorting recycling)
Walking the dog (although see my earlier comment on *Walking blank time*)	

2. In your notebook, write your blank time everyday task.

3. Before you start, put your phone in another room or in a drawer, somewhere you won't be tempted to pick it up and disengage with blank time.

4. If that seems a challenge, promise yourself you can use your phone after the ten minutes of blank time is over.

5. Don't try to focus on anything as you work. Let your mind go where it will. The movement and the mind-wandering mode will enable you to unfrazzle, and your brain to sub-consciously work through issues and problems, plus sift and sort the events of the day, or clear the slate for the day to come.

6. Repeat with the same or another task the next day, again for the first ten minutes.

7. Aim for every day this week.

Recommendations

Choose in advance what your everyday task will be. It will help you to enter blank time if you've already made that decision. If you need extra help to focus, use the tools in *Create an Unfrazzle bubble* after this section.

Managing blank time

Apart from that human tendency to disrupt blank time – perhaps because of stress hormones, dopamine need, or guilt over appearing to do nothing, there are two other reasons that may challenge your engagement with blank time: other people, and the world around you.

1. Other people
If you're in blank time – whether that's staring out of a train window, walking down a street, or doing an everyday task, it may look as if you're 'available'. Other people won't mean to disrupt your Unfrazzle opportunity, but it happens, because you don't look as if you're doing anything in particular. Explaining yourself in advance can help, but not everybody will understand or be aware of your need to free your brain.

2. The world around you
Brain-frazzling stimuli is everywhere: on public transport recorded voices spell out every bus or station stop. Your walk may involve dodging through crowds, traffic and advertisements. The neighbours' radio or conversations might interrupt your blank time everyday tasks. Dogs bark, builders clank, horns beep.

You can't prevent the world or the people around you from doing their thing, but you can minimise the impact it has on your sense of peace.

Exercise: Create an Unfrazzle bubble

I love being a part of the world, letting birdsong drift overhead and lifting my face to the sky. I also relish the opportunity for random connections with strangers. However, when we live in a noisy, stimulating urban environment we need blank time more than ever, and birdsong can be hard to hear.
Creating an Unfrazzle bubble around you will enable the world to bounce off the bubble, rather than the blank time within.

Firstly:

Think of what the challenge is to your blank time in particular situations: *Other people* or *The world around you.*

1. *Other people*
This exercise will send a *"do not disturb"* message to the world.
Choose your Unfrazzle bubble of choice – or go for a combination. Wear these to create your bubble.

- Baseball caps (or any brimmed hat that shades your eyes).
- Hooded tops.
- Sunglasses.
- Headphones, or earbuds that are obviously visible. You don't

have to connect them to anything, because their presence will send a message that you are unavailable.

2. *The world around you*

a) To block out some visual stimuli, wear **caps / brimmed hats** or **sunglasses**: think blinkers on a horse.

b) To block auditory stimuli, put one or more of the following tracks on your player:

White noise (cuts out conversational sound – other colours / types work at different frequencies so adapt according to your need).

Classical music – slow and romantic is better.

Any music without strong hooks – it must be music that your brain does not need to pay attention to.

Extra tips:

- Do you have an old-style MP3 player with no internet connection? Listen to your tracks on this so you won't be tempted to use your phone as you engage with blank time.
- Otherwise, put your phone on flight mode for the duration.

vi) Sink into Unfrazzle: tips for extra blank time

Below are some ideas for extra blank time. They are extras: you'll see that most of them can't be a part of the everyday routine. Some require funds. However, if you're willing and able to try them, you might find one or two that give you the acreage of space you need to properly unwind, even if you can't afford a fortnight in the Tuscan countryside or a month on a Thai beach.

Floatation

A floatation tank looks like a giant egg, or a pod from a science fiction film. It is designed to give you complete sensory deprivation for an hour, to enable your mind to unhook and calm down from stimuli and stress.

Each tank is filled with a warm bath of Epsom salts which enables you to float. When you climb in, the lid is lowered and if you wish, you can float in complete darkness (there are also LED lights you can switch on if that seems too much).

After an hour (you can raise the lid earlier if you wish), you climb out and shower off the salt.

> **Daisy is an ex-DJ from Cork in Ireland. Her Unfrazzle of choice is a floatation tank.**
> I was listening to music so much, at such a high volume, that I developed tinnitus and hyperacusis [a hyper-sensitivity to sound]. As a consequence, I became super-stressed if I was near anyone talking too loudly, or repetitive music beats were playing within hearing distance.
> I started seeing an audiologist to rehabilitate my sound

> tolerance, and at the same time a practitioner recommended floatation.
>
> I still don't really know why, but something about it transformed my fear levels when I was inside. It's not exactly quiet, but my hearing becomes attuned to my heartbeat and the sound of my breathing. I feel as if everything inside me just calms down. Any time now that I feel too over-revved, I have a float and it sorts me out.

Floatation might be perfect for you, or it might not be what you need right now. If you're scared of enclosed spaces, there are larger tanks you can try instead, which are open to the room rather than with a closed lid. Every time I've tried floatation, I've had a different response, depending on how I felt before I went in. When I was really stressed out, my mind was literally unable to slow down for a moment the entire hour. However much to my surprise, when I came out I felt astonishingly calmer. It happened *despite* my racing brain.

I believe that the movement of water lapping around your body gives you just enough stimuli so that you can engage with blank time (more unfrazzling than mind-wandering alone).

It might not transform your life as it did Daisy's, but if you can afford the £40-£50 per session, you might discover it's what you need.

Epsom salts bath

What you'll need: Epsom salts, candles, bath oil

Can't afford, or live nowhere near, a floatation tank? Then create your own version at home. You won't be able to float in your bathtub, but Epsom salts detoxify your skin and can feel very soothing.

Run a bath to your temperature and pour in up to one cupful of Epsom salts. Add your favourite bath oil and light as many candles as you can. Turn off the light and climb in. Allow yourself no outside stimuli while in the bath: no book, no light apart from candlelight, and certainly no phone or other device.

Twenty minutes in a hot bath will enable your body to sweat and excrete toxins, although the point here is to get you into blank time. Again, the gentle movement of water, and the slight stimuli from candlelight, will engage your mind with blank time.

Get your hair cut

If you're forced to listen to the radio at high volume, or talk to the hairdresser, while getting your hair cut, it'll be hard to engage with blank time. Additionally, if you're worried about whether you're getting a feathered look rather than the blunt cut you asked for, you'll find it difficult to allow your mind to drift.

However, if the music and other chatter is background enough, and if your hairdresser understands that you don't want to talk, you'll have a good opportunity to engage with blank time. You'll be unable to pick up your phone while your hair's being cut, and the sensory input involved, as the hairdresser touches your head and lifts your hair, will, if the moment is right, get you into blank time.

It's also the sort of blank time you don't have to add in. If it happens, it happens. A good hairdresser will understand when you'd rather sit quietly, and although some salons up the energy in the room, others try to create a calmer, more nurturing atmosphere.

Go on a silent retreat

However, if you *really* want to engage with blank time, and you have a spare few hundred pounds, go on a silent retreat. Many are run following Buddhist tradition, and although there may be plenty of meditation sessions, you will also get the opportunity to walk or move around without having to engage in chatter. Letting the mind speak to itself can be a very strange experience at first, but the growing popularity of silent retreats suggests that they may be hugely beneficial for anyone who feels overwhelmed with the noise of the world.

Stare at a fire

And finally, the next time you are camping, or sitting in front of a log or coal fire, give yourself as long as you need to stare into the flames, allowing your eyes to follow its flickering. Fire is the elemental human blank time, practised for millennia, where the stimuli from the flames matches the mind-wandering mode, and gives the brain a moment for reflection and peace.

Chapter Four summed up

What is blank time?

It combines the *mind-wandering network,* when the brain has no external task to focus on, with *minor stimuli for the body or brain.*

What will it do for me?

It will heal and unfrazzle you.

How does blank time unfrazzle?

- It gives the brain a break from constantly receiving incoming stimuli, which is fatiguing work.
- It will enable you to take a bird's eye view of life, and gain perspective.
- It will enable you to make decisions and solve problems.
- In addition, because of the space you get, blank time might enable you to come up with genius ideas.

Why you might avoid blank time:

- It can create space for uncomfortable thoughts and emotions.
- You might love feeling the exhilaration of stress.
- All humans are drawn to chasing dopamine.
- You might feel guilty with 'nothing' to do.

How life in the modern world eliminates blank time:

1. To get people to spend money, their attention is required. Blank time is a *lack* of attention, and we live in a profit-driven world.

2. Busy city life, despite its huge benefits, is highly stimulating, and eliminates blank time.

How can blank time unfrazzle me in my day-to-day life?

By turning the everyday grind of routines into opportunities to engage with blank time.

The everyday blank time routines

Aim for 3x 10-minute sessions every day, and build from there. Build a combination of:

- Public transport blank time
- Walking blank time
- Everyday tasks blank time

In a nutshell:

If you want to feel more unfrazzled every day, put blank time into your daily life, and make it part of your already-existing routines.

CHAPTER FIVE

DEEPER UNFRAZZLE: HOW TO RECONNECT

You're intelligent. Don't ask me how I know, I can tell. Remember the 'clever' brain I talked about in previous chapters? The part of us that analyses, makes decisions, sequences, uses logic, and so on. All intelligent people are highly connected to their clever brain – and rightly so.

I'm sure you also remember that when you're frazzled your clever brain starts malfunctioning: you make poor choices, are unable to prioritise, and all the rest. Of the emotional consequences of frazzle you'll be well aware: feeling anxious, stressed, unrested, wired, irritable, fed up, and more.

To get out of frazzle and into Unfrazzle, it's ultra important to embrace imperfection and do less stuff. It's also vital to get control of your phone usage, plus take an hour before bed to enter the Wind-Down Zone. And to get space and time for yourself, recalibrate your everyday routines for ten-minute chunks of thrice-daily blank time.

But there is one more thing, and – as I've discovered – it's vital for a deeper Unfrazzle.

Many people who are highly connected to their clever brain have also, over the years, become less connected to the rest of themselves. That's certainly true of me, and perhaps you're like that, perhaps not. On the next page you can take the quiz to find out how 'clever-brained' you are (and how less connected you are to other brain areas).

We often hear about how important it is to engage with the whole of us, and in this chapter you'll find out how to use the senses as a way to get into that engagement. You'll discover why it's important to connect with the whole brain, and how doing that will get you into Unfrazzle.

You'll hear how I went from despair to revelation, when I worked out an easy way to get into mindfulness. You'll also hear from people both in detention, and outside, on how they connect with both mindful awareness and the senses. You'll discover how this reconnection works in alternation with the default, mind-wandering mode of the brain (which you explored in Chapter Four) in order to unfrazzle more deeply.

You'll learn how to reconnect to the senses in the everyday *Unfrazzle* way – by incorporating it into your already-existing routines, just as you did with blank time in the last chapter. This time, you'll discover how to add it on to at least one daily blank time routine, and how to turn an everyday activity into an everyday treat, via a reconnection with one or more of the senses.

As with the previous chapters, there's always more to explore in reconnection, via a weekly or monthly deeper Unfrazzle. I'll end with tips on ways to get a deeper connection to the whole body, if you have the time, space, and the funds to do so.

i) Disconnected

Quiz: Are you a clever-brain person?

Read the questions and write the answers in your notebook.

1. How long do you spend every day, on average, at a computer?

a) less than 30 minutes
b) 30 minutes to an hour
c) over an hour

2. Look at the list below. To what extent does your working life involve *any* of the following?

Planning
Task-switching (often known as multi-tasking)
Decision-making
Responsibility for others
Strategic / logical / sequential / analytical thinking
Problem-solving

a) less than 10%
b) between 10 and 30%
c) over 30%

3. Do you read books or articles (whether in paper or digital format)?

a) Only this one
b) Hardly ever
c) Fairly regularly

4. Are you a questioning person?

a) No
b) I've never thought about it
c) Yes

5. Do you eat quickly?

a) Never
b) Sometimes
c) I have no idea

6. When you're involved in a task, do you ever forget to eat / drink water / go to the toilet?

a) No, never
b) Sometimes
c) I don't know

7. Could you draw the front of your house or building from memory?

a) I could draw with lots of accurate detail
b) I'd draw the front door with accurate detail, the rest more vaguely
c) It would be a rough sketch

8. Is your posture *right now* balanced, or slumped?

a) I always make sure my posture is in balance
b) I'm sitting properly *now* (maybe I wasn't before)
c) I'm not sure

9. Do you sing?

a) Yes, every day
b) Sometimes
c) Only when I have to

10. When you do exercise or other physical activity, what happens?

a) I remain 100% focused inside my body
b) I connect to my body
c) I dip in and out of focus

Now add up your totals for A, B and C answers
Questions 1-4 focus on how clever-brained you are. **Questions 5-10** focus on how connected you are to your whole self.

Mostly As
You're an intelligent person who's learned to live in the whole of you, not just your clever brain. If you're frazzled, however, then look at where you scored **Bs** and **Cs** in **Questions 5-10**. Disengaging from your clever brain in these areas, and returning to an engagement with the whole of you, will help you to unfrazzle. Read the rest of this chapter to discover how.

Mostly Bs

You're a clever-brain person who's made some changes in order to reconnect with yourself. Again, look at the final six questions as a focus for where you can move into the **As** to connect even further. This chapter will get you towards this.

Mostly Cs

Your clever brain is always switched on, like mine. You approach life in a spirit of critical engagement, which has allowed you to understand what lies beneath the surface of things, and has expanded your horizons. On the other hand, you'd definitely benefit from a whole-self, whole-brain reconnection.

Note that being clever-brained does *not* mean being frazzled. You don't have to dumb yourself down, stop reading or get an under-stimulating job in order to unfrazzle. However, reconnecting with the whole of you, not just your clever brain, *will* help you if you *are* frazzled.

Get reconnected

As babies, we were intimately connected to the whole of ourselves. We expressed ourselves when we were hungry, thirsty, tired. We wiggled our fingers and our toes. We felt from inside our bodies. We drank milk; we slept; we saw; we heard.

Over time, as our clever brain developed, we became less connected to the whole of us. Our clever brain operates mainly via the prefrontal cortex. This is the area that lies at the front of the brain, and is what makes us human.

People who are highly connected to their clever brain – analytical, questioning, educated, 'thinky' people – have often become disconnected from a **true** engagement with other brain areas. (In this instance, I am not talking about the emotional brain, which I mentioned in Chapter Two, but other areas).

For example, think about the last meal you ate. Did you focus fully on the eating of it, or were you doing something else at the same time? Were you at your computer, or talking, or running to the shops? When animals eat, they focus fully on the eating; they don't try to do two things at once.

Most of us are not fully engaged with what we're doing – unless what we're doing involves our clever brain: and that's the part we most often need to rest.

Each act you do is controlled by areas of your brain, although not in isolation. Networks across the cortex light up when you engage in different actions. Focusing fully on an area that's *not* your clever brain will create strong connections, and will give your clever brain a rest. If your mind is constantly split, and if you don't connect to the whole of yourself, those connections will be under-engaged and weak. The stronger the networks connecting your clever brain, and the weaker the others, the more likely you are to analyse, plan, consider, revise – and less likely you are to be fully in the moment of what you're doing.

Resting the clever brain doesn't mean you'll become stupid: it's frazzle that will do that. *Every* brain area needs just the right amount of work and rest – not too much, not too little, just like Goldilocks. Any brain area below can start malfunctioning, if the emotional brain gets involved and starts sending *danger! danger!* messages throughout the body.

This chapter, however, focuses on rehabilitating the clever brain, because it is in resetting its workload that a deeper Unfrazzle is found.

Brain areas

Frontal lobe: This houses the prefrontal cortex. It enables us to suppress impulses, be motivated (it contains most of our dopamine neurons), and it activates our muscles.

Temporal lobe: This gives us our sense of smell, hearing, sound, emotions and memory.

Parietal lobe: This enables us to perceive physical sensations such as touch.

Cerebellum: This co-ordinates our muscles and enables our balance.

What happens when you're frazzled

People who are clever-brained yet frazzled often try to 'think' their way out of frazzle using the prefrontal cortex. They analyse what's wrong, make plans, sequence, detail it down, work it all out. But doing that doesn't lead to Unfrazzle – in fact, it can make things worse.

Blank time frees your brain from fatiguing prefrontal cortex work. That alone will get you into an Unfrazzle state, where your prefrontal cortex has space to do all that planning, come up with all those amazing ideas – and have a rest.

However, to deeply unfrazzle, you need to not only stop fatiguing the prefrontal cortex, you need to work the other areas of your brain too. It's the same as resting a strained muscle, and building up the muscles around it. Resting is OK, but if you work to build the surrounding tissue, you won't damage it again.

Therefore, connecting with the whole of yourself, giving a workout to those other lobes of the brain and building them up as you would a weakened muscle, will truly calm you down, and get you into deep, healing Unfrazzle.

ii) The mindfulness connection

About mindfulness

You've probably heard of mindfulness by now. Perhaps you've tried it, or perhaps you have a daily practice. But in case you don't know much about it, mindfulness is a meditation practice developed from Buddhist tradition. It is also a way of seeing the world, and a way of being. It can be in a tiny action or moment, or it can be the essence of someone's existence.

Basically, it means being fully in the moment of what the body is doing, feeling or experiencing. To be mindful is to be fully aware of one's actions and processes, without judgement and without getting caught up in ideas, dreams, opinions, plans. It is the opposite of the mind-wandering mode we discover during blank time: it is focused.

In mindful meditation, you observe thoughts and feelings coming and going without getting involved with them. It's often likened to watching leaves drift down the stream. If you get caught up in a thought, step out of the stream and watch the flow drift past.

Mindful awareness enables us to connect with our whole selves, and a regular practice of mindful meditation has been proven[6] to reduce depression and stress in some people by rewiring the brain.

It's no surprise that mindfulness is often used as a tool to help the frazzled. Yet even though it's been found to be life-changing, it is also extremely challenging, because all of us have what's often known as the "monkey mind".

---

6   https://scholar.harvard.edu/sara_lazar

What is the monkey mind?

It's a metaphor to describe our brain as it swings from thought to thought, often without giving us peace. At times we need to be mentally active, and at others we need to rest: but monkeys are naughty, and won't do as we tell them.

When we need to rest, our monkey mind won't let us relax. It dips into the future and back to the past; it uses our prefrontal cortex to plan and scheme and dream and judge and worry and hope.

Because it's naughty, it's often when we most need to clear the mind of debris that it pops up and starts jabbering away at us: and if we are frazzled, stressed, anxious, fearful, then mindful meditation can be more challenging, because our monkey mind becomes more active than usual, jabbing us with to-do lists, future fears, past regrets, problems and questions.

Test yourself: Mindfulness & the monkey mind

After you have read this, you're going to close your eyes for around two minutes. During that time, focus on thoughts and sensations coming and going, without getting caught up in meaning, interpretation, or mind-wandering. If you notice your-self getting caught up, step back and observe the thoughts going past. When you have finished, open your eyes and read on.

Ready? Good luck.

Test results

Welcome back. How did you do? Take a moment to think back on your experience, and then read what your answers say about you.

The skipper

You've skipped the exercise and have come straight to the answers. Perhaps you think you can do it, or you definitely know you can't. I'm a total skipper too, and it's my monkey mind stopping me – and you – from focusing fully. The exercises in this chapter will be so useful as a baseline way into stilling the non-stop mind.

The tryer

You tried the exercise – perhaps not for a full two minutes, but you gave it a go. Your mind hopped and skittered about, getting caught up in thoughts, returning to focus, and then jumping off again. This is totally normal for everyone, even for people who have a regular mindfulness practice. We all have off-days and on-days; it doesn't mean a thing. The exercises in the chapter will give you an easier, more practical way to remain in focus.

The practitioner

More or less, you were able to remain fully in the moment for two minutes. If you're able to do this, then you're already practised at mindful awareness. Perhaps you utilised some techniques you've learned from your practice – a focus on the breath or a body scan (this is where you focus the attention on each area of the body in turn). The exercises will give you a thrice-daily practice that won't make you commit more time than you already give.

The problem with mindfulness

The greatest challenge to using mindfulness to live a calmer, less frazzled life is that it takes time and effort, with a daily practice, in order to calm that monkey mind.

One of the reasons I came to writing this book is because for anyone who is really frazzled, mindfulness can feel like a mountain we can't even begin to climb. It can also feel a bit 'hippyish' for anyone who's not used to this sort of practice.

This is why Chapter Five of *Unfrazzle* isn't mindfulness as such, but a version with the process stripped back to basics, and a practice that won't require you to add an extra to your everyday life (as with all the routines in the book, it lies in something you already do).

Even people who are practised at mindfulness can forget the fundamentals of Unfrazzle (such as getting control of your phone, for example). It's why I use blank time as key to unfrazzle, even though it's the opposite of mindfulness. Your monkey mind can run riot during blank time, and it will still help you to unfrazzle.

I've experienced for myself that aiming for true mindfulness can feed into my high-achieving tendencies, and I can't be the only one. Not only that, but a busy city-centre environment holds many more challenges to mindful calm than atop a Tibetan hillside. I found that out the hard way.

Mindfulness and me: Part one

Deep into the crisis, as you now know, I was suffering a huge amount of stress, frazzled to the point of being unable to decide between two jars of olives. I'd also begun that perfectionist wellness journey I talked about in Chapter One. As I researched and sought help, and went for anything going, I was offered a mindfulness course, which I signed up to gleefully. I'd heard so much about it, and I knew how mindfulness had really helped friends of mine. Here it was, on a taught course, and I would learn finally how to put all that frazzle behind me and become the blissed-out person I knew I was inside: or at least get a vital route map that would take me there.

Apart from the meetings, we had daily homework of mindful meditations to listen to, a different one each week. They covered various aspects of mindful awareness, such as a body scan, a silent meditation and a movement meditation. One week the meditation was on noticing the sound around us, again with a non-judgemental awareness of any thoughts or feelings.

It was during a brutal heatwave in the middle of a busy city. I sat in my living room overlooking the main road, with all the windows open and the afternoon sun streaming through. All I could hear was the non-stop rumble of cars and lorries passing by below. The traffic noise was so loud I couldn't even hear the meditation.

I'd learned in the course that it was OK to feel frustrated, to notice it without judgement, that everything was a process. I tried to do that, then got up and went into the bedroom, lying on the bed with my earphones in.

I listened to the soothing voice. *Notice any sounds around you. Perhaps a birdsong. Perhaps there is no sound, and notice the absence of sound too.*

In my case, *notice* was a redundant instruction. There was nothing I could do *but* notice the sounds around me, despite the earphones and the soothing voice. Our neighbours had started their Saturday night early, and party music was thumping into the air. From experience, I knew this would continue for another twelve hours or so, becoming louder and more raucous as the night wore on.

From the rooftops came the shrill calls of summer seagulls

mating, and from his garden another neighbour held a monologue on his mobile phone, his voice amplified by the walls of the buildings around.

The instruction to notice sound meant that all the usual urban commotion slammed up against my brain. I may have been able to disassociate from it before, but my high stress levels meant that I suddenly felt surrounded by a relentless tide of discordant noise. *Absence of sound,* I thought bitterly. *Very funny.*

I felt more trapped and less calm than I had before I started. I tore my earphones out and sobbed into my pillow while the noise continued around me, unabated.

What mindfulness taught me

Living in the middle of a busy, thriving city, despite its benefits, meant I was surrounded by so much sound stimuli that when I was in the middle of a crisis, all of that noise became overwhelming. Mindfulness brought me into an even closer awareness of that sound, making it even more overwhelming, and adding to my frustration because I was trying so hard to remain calm.

However, that mindfulness course gave me an essential grounding in the basics of mindful awareness, and started me on the path I am on today. At the time, it felt like attaching a sticking plaster to a gaping wound, but it was in searching for a way to discover stillness in a hectic urban environment that led me to writing this chapter.

Not only that: in essence, mindful awareness has enormous benefits for our wellbeing, if we can access it within the everyday. Plenty of books and apps exist to help us do that. Mine has taken you here via the Unfrazzle route, and my aim is that if you've laid the groundwork with the exercises in the previous four chapters, you'll be better able to reconnect with yourself using the exercises here.

Mark is a recent convert to his own method of meditation. He lives in East London.

I started trying Vedic and transcendental meditation about two years ago as a way to still my constantly jumping-about mind. I find it hard to focus on one project or one thought at a time, and I'm always moving on to the next thing.

The more I've practised meditation, the more I've worked out how to let go of trying to still the mind, and just notice the thoughts as they come and go. Your expectations become lower, the more you do it, and the more it becomes part of the everyday routine, like brushing your teeth.

If you'd told me a few years ago I'd be meditating daily, I'd have laughed. It wasn't ever part of my identity. I would always relax with alcohol, in the pub, surrounded by friends. Not that there's anything wrong with that, but now I've added in mediation too, and it's changed my life.

iii) Get into the senses

Detention stories – the class

This morning, the classroom is full of people occupied with different activities. Our creative theme this week is "Life", and at the table by the window, Jian is making a plasticine planet Earth, moulding the clay with his hands and rolling out slivers of green. Opposite him Abi is following step-by-step instructions to draw a simple flower, creating shoots and petals from the white of the paper.

Sitting at the central table near me is Cal. He only arrived yesterday, and is in a state of jittery high stress. He doesn't speak much English and hasn't the brain space to learn any right now. I met him an hour ago, brought in by one of his room-mates, and I noticed he was in a state of emergency stress. I sat him down, put a colouring activity in front of him and a pack of brightly-coloured pens. He is still sitting there, colouring in the page before him. I doubt he has a clue what he is doing, but he is fully focused, keeping his brain and hands occupied with the simple act of filling in white spaces with colour.

Colouring in won't remove his troubles, but it will calm his brain while it processes everything that has happened to him so far.

Peter is fluent in English and is highly educated. He's writing a poem with the theme of "Life", trying out phrases and rolling them around his mouth before committing them to paper. When he's finished, he'll read it aloud for the sound of the words as they emerge, and then I'll type it up to be displayed on the classroom wall.

Dev was unable to attend school in his own country, and cannot read or write his native language. Therefore he finds forming the letters of the Roman alphabet difficult, and so he is engaged in tracing a sequence of Cs, and pronouncing the sound while reading different words: cat, cap, can. Meanwhile, my core group of ESOL learners is engaged with studying vocabulary. As an experiment, I've brought in a few spices for them to smell and guess what they are. It drifts into a discussion about food, and their favourite dishes. Baz returns to the packet of cumin and tells me a story about his childhood. The cumin seeds spill everywhere as he gestures, filling the classroom with their scent.

Full focus & the senses

In detention, mindful awareness is pretty much an impossibility. For people in a state of emergency or high stress, getting into a mindfully calm state is like travelling to the moon.

For people such as Hossain, who I wrote about in Chapter Four, his highly-stressed, malfunctioning brain means he finds it impossible to focus on anything. When people get unwanted removal directions, or another piece of bad news, they can hardly sit still for five minutes, never mind concentrate on a longer task and complete it.

Yet if they are able to fully focus, and are able to participate in one or more finite activities, they discover it is a form of escape. For a few minutes or a few hours they are no longer 'detainees'. They are not a label – whether that's one of their own or someone else's. They are in the moment, being.

We none of us are any different. Full focus has the potential to help us all: at the same time, it's tricky to do. It's why I've found that engaging the brain with one or more of the senses is a way into full focus for highly stressed people.

For example, colouring in works another part of the brain rather than the prefrontal cortex. It's not planning or sequencing. However, a (prefrontal cortex-related) decision has to be made to use certain colours, and I use colour-by-numbers for people who find that decision making difficult. Personally, I prefer colour-by-numbers to regular colouring in, because it's one less decision for me to make. However, many of the guys come from cultures that are deeply embedded with an appreciation of colour, with clear, deep routes in their brain for colour choices, and so find that aspect easier to access.

Making plasticine sculptures uses the sense of touch, and drawing uses touch (pencil on paper), sound (of the pencil), and the visual sense. Scents are evocative, can unlock memories, and can help to pull the brain away from difficult sensations such as pain. The rhythm and sounds of words, such as those found in poetic language, for example, can help to focus the mind away from its usual everyday stress. Using the visual and touch senses via tracing letters and following simple words is a simple way for people who do not know the Roman alphabet – especially people who have extensive literacy needs – to focus their mind on the basics.

The truth about multi-tasking

Full focus basically means *not multi-tasking.*

Full focus means focusing on one task, completely, in order to finish it, and then moving on to the next.

I used to be proud of my ability to multi-task. I thought it was a special skill (like my 'skill' of being very busy). I could juggle many balls, spin many plates, keep a dozen things in my brain at the same time.

During that crisis, I often gave off the appearance of being not just capable, but superhumanly capable. I know, because many people told me so. I enjoyed giving that impression, even while on the side suffering paralysing attacks of fear so great I became almost totally frozen. Even when I was operating in the world, doing ten things 'at once' (something that, as you'll see, is impossible), I liked the look of appearing as if in control of everything – despite, like a dog in the ocean, the frantic paddling of my feet below the waves.

I now see that ability as both a tendency – and, sometimes, a necessity. On occasion, 'multi-tasking' is inevitable (you'll find out in the next section why I'm putting that in air quotes). At work, in the scenario above, I have to keep focus on many different people, with different needs, doing different activities. Any of us who have a busy home or work life, with many hats to wear, will know this only too well.

But what happens is that my – and perhaps your – ability to juggle those balls bleeds into areas where *it's not actually necessary.* It becomes a habit that's hard to put down. It's time to get real: that so-called special skill is one mammoth frazzler for our overworked brain.

Mini-exercise: Are you a multi-tasker?

Go back to the *Everyday grind* quiz at the beginning of Chapter Four. Many of these answers are about our habit of multi-tasking. Read again which answers you chose, and add up your score below:

Question	a)	b)	c)
1	3	0	0
2	0	3	0
3	3	3	0
4	0	3	0
5	0	3	0
6	0	3	0
7	0	0	0
8	0	3	0
9	3	3	0
10	0	3	0

Out of a maximum of **27 points, how many did you get?**

The more points you scored, the more of a multi-tasker you are. Anything over half (13 points) makes you an habitual multi-tasker. But you probably know whether you have a tendency to do many things at the same time.

How so-called 'multi-tasking' frazzles

Instead of reaping the big rewards that come from sustained, focused effort, we instead reap empty rewards from completing a thousand little sugarcoated tasks.

Daniel Levitin, The Organized Mind

Neuroscientist Daniel Levitin has studied both the realities of so-called 'multi-tasking', and its effects on the brain. Basically, when you focus on a task, you utilise a network in the brain known as the *central executive*. It uses the prefrontal cortex, amongst other areas. It's the top-level, high-powered managing director of the brain, and switching it on uses a lot of brain fuel.

Every time you turn to a task, you activate the central executive. Then, if you turn to another task, it switches on again. Then, even if you return to your initial task, it activates a third time. Each time the central executive is activated, brain fuel is used up, giving you that 'tired brain' feeling. Not only that, but multi-tasking increases the production of those stress hormones, cortisol and adrenaline. As you already know, an overload of stress hormones causing havoc in the body = symptoms of frazzle.

Multi-tasking is actually *task-switching*. Each time you flip activities you use up more brain fuel and release more stress into your system. Because you can be drawn towards those stress hormones (they make everybody feel more alive) you can be drawn towards multi-tasking even when juggling many balls is not necessary, and depletes you.

In addition, smartphones contain a vortex of potential tasks that you can switch to easily. If you see somebody on their phone flipping from a train times app, to an online shopping site, to a social media feed, to a photo, to a message, and then back, each time they press a button their brain becomes progressively more stressed and more tired.

How not to multi-task

i) Ask the question: Is this task necessary?
Embrace the principle of Unfrazzle, *Do less stuff.* Less multi-tasking (or task-switching) means you'll use up less brain fuel and release fewer stress hormones into your body.

Getting into the habit of asking yourself *is it necessary?* is a hard one for those of us who have a tendency to multi-task. That's why embracing the whole of Unfrazzle, including the two principles and all the exercises, will help to rewire the brain away from seeking to multi-task.

ii) Group tasks together and do them one after another

Busy day ahead? Categorise tasks into distinct groups, and then do them one at a time. For example, group your *kitchen-based tasks* together, and do them one after another, after another. Putting food shopping away, then washing up, then preparing food, then cooking.

Similarly, group your *email/office-based tasks* together, and maybe *kids-to-bed* (or similar) *based tasks.*

Switching between checking emails to washing up to putting on the TV for the news to taking down the laundry to texting your friend back to sorting the recycling is – obviously – going to frazzle you much more than doing *the same category of tasks one after another.*

It's taken me a long time to change my behaviour, especially after a full day of divided attention at work in a busy class. Even after all those neuroscience books, and a decision to face up to reality, I still sometimes find it hard to focus on one task at a time.

However, I've found a method that's not just helped, but has been fundamental in pulling my brain back from that fractured-attention frazzle. I've realised that although *not* doing something can be helpful, it's even more helpful to do something. And to rid ourselves of the multi-tasking habit, it's this:

iii) Get connected to your whole brain

Multi-tasking utilises the prefrontal cortex, the part of our brain that gets easily frazzled. As we've seen, there are other brain areas that control our senses and, although we use them in a basic way – to see, smell, hear, touch, taste – we often rarely engage with them in a full, complete sense.

Connecting with our full brain – our whole self – means we are less likely to multi-task, and will be able to develop an ability to focus completely.

One of the many benefits of neuroplasticity is that working to fully focus on (for example) engaging with our sense of taste means that we'll also be able to fully focus on another, unrelated task – writing a novel, cooking dinner, speaking to a loved one – without the fractured attention of frazzle. Imagine being able to be fully present in the moment of what you're doing – playing with a child, celebrating a friend's birthday, having a picnic in the park, without a ticker-tape of to-do lists and worries running through your mind. Not only that, but imagine you can achieve that *without* telling yourself to 'enjoy' or 'be present' in the moment. There's nothing more guaranteed to ensure that you won't enjoy a moment than telling yourself to enjoy it (I know, I've been there).

Your present-ness, or your enjoyment, will happen *anyway*. If you're able to sustain a fully-focused engagement with the senses on a regular basis – the routine for which I'll explain in this chapter – you'll find yourself effortlessly enjoying that picnic or that birthday without thinking of a million other things. Remember the childhood you, who could spend hours (so it seemed) watching an ant crawl across a patch of grass, or fully relish a moment without thinking of anything else? That's all in there, waiting to be reclaimed, once you can get into that whole-brain connection.

Remember: using the prefrontal cortex to plan, schedule, analyse, strategise and problem-solve is a positive aspect of being human. But using that prefrontal cortex to 'think' our way out of frazzle will only get us so far. Getting into the senses will lead us the rest of the way, to a deep Unfrazzle.

The senses: from the beginning

Despite my calamitous experience with the sound-focus meditation, the grounding in mindfulness I received helped me with understanding how to get hold of calm in the middle of chaos. It also taught me how useful a focus on the senses is as a way in to connecting with our whole selves.

My experience with the sound focus – and the other meditations – also taught me that when we are frazzled and live in a challenging environment, we need to start with the awareness of those challenges in mind. In the exercises that follow this one, you'll see how I adapted what I learned from the course to make it work for me, living on a main road surrounded by people and noise, commuting and working with people at the severe edge of critical stress.

If those exercises work for me – and they do, with plenty of practice – then they can work for anyone. Engaging with the whole of ourselves, all of our brain, is a lifelong journey. If you are already practised at mindful awareness you may well know when, where and how you find that full engagement more challenging. That 'edge' – the difficult place – is the starting point for the everyday reconnection I talk about here.

Whole-self connection using the senses

This whole-self, whole-brain connection is *micro*. It lies in a complete focus on small details.

Visual sense – the details of what you see around you.

Auditory sense – the individual sounds you hear.

Taste sense – holding a taste in your mouth to absorb all its details.

Smell sense – noticing every faint smell in the air.

Bodily sense – the connection of your skin to its external environment (such as clothes, or the sense of feet on the ground), but also an *inner* bodily sense – the curvature of your spine, the muscles at your core.

Exercise: Three ways to connect to the senses

There is no 'right' way to engage mindfully with the senses. From day to day, even minute to minute, we are different people with different needs at each moment.

Below are three exercises to connect to the senses. Don't pressurise yourself as you do them. See them as an experiment, a moment to work out how each one feels for you, right now.

Exercise 1: Quick-fire sense rotation

> This is a good exercise for when a stress wave hits. You know what I mean: a battering of overwhelm or anxiety, a jabbering thought loop, or something else. Doing it quickly will switch your brain off its old track and onto a different route.
> In the following exercise, rotate all five senses quickly, focusing on one detail each time, returning to the first and rotating again.

- Don't linger on any one sense for too long. Aim for one breath in, and one breath out, with each sense. If you don't connect to the breath, that's fine too.
- Make sure each time that you home in on a detail.
- It can be the same detail you return to, again and again, or it can be different, whatever comes to mind first.
- This will stop your analytical, clever brain getting involved, which is antithetical to mindful awareness.

For example:
Visual – a tiny mark on the windowsill next to me.
Auditory – the sound of birdsong nearby.
Smell – the scent of fresh air through the window.
Taste – the lingering aftertaste of black coffee.
Bodily sense – my rounded shoulders as I type

Do this now, for a minimum of one rotation. It will not take you longer than a minute.
If a stress-wave hits, do this sense-rotation over and over until you feel calmer once more.

Exercise 2: One sense focus

If you would rather not focus on all the senses – perhaps because some of them are uncomfortable for you right now – then instead you can focus on one neutral sense alone. When I was surrounded by the noise of neighbours and seagulls, I could have focused instead on my bodily sense, going into every detail of it. Choose a sense to home in on. If you feel comfortable to close your eyes, try the bodily sense.

Home in on details. It doesn't matter what details, or how many.
Aim for one breath with each detail. But if you can't connect to the breath, it doesn't matter.

Example: focus on the bodily sense

- Try your outer body first. Focus on its position and the feel of clothes against your skin.
- Then try your inner body, for example the muscles at your core. Your stomach digesting food. The hair on your head. The connection of your bones and the straightness of your spine.
- It doesn't matter how many areas you focus on. There is no 'right' way to do it.

Example: focus on the visual sense

- Look right down in front of you. Home in on the smallest detail you can see.
- Then go to another detail, then another, then another.
- If comment, analysis, judgement or any clever-brain thinking creeps in, go to another detail.

Do this for ten breaths of ten visual details.

Exercise 3: Deepest focus

For a deeper, more restful connection, this exercise will enable you to sink into a full-focus engagement as you would a warm bath, by giving another brain area a proper workout.

Our attention is often drawn to difficult sensations, such as pain in the body, or uncomfortable sounds, smells or sights. Yet there is often an area – or many areas – within that sense that is neutral. Connecting to those areas is not automatic, because the brain wants to alert us to difficulties in order to prepare us for fight-or-flight.

I find doing this within the taste, visual or the bodily sense the most useful, because we often do not have a choice of sounds or smells to choose from. If you're sitting in a café as you read this, with music playing and people talking nearby, you might prefer to home out of sound rather than in.

Similarly, someone else's perfume, or the smell of fuel, cleaning products or other things beyond your control can take over your olfactory sense.

However, if it feels available to you, you can try focusing on one particular smell or sound, letting it soak into your being without analysis or comment.

Visual sense

When I commute to work, I'm surrounded by details that draw my attention and yet are uncomfortable – flashing lights, advertising, people. Instead of allowing my brain to engage with it all, I look down at the ground. As I wait for my train, I focus in on the minute detail of the cracks in the concrete at my feet.

Home in on *one* detail in front of you. Go as small as you possibly can.

For example:

- Pay close attention to the grain in the wood of the table.
- Trace the veins of a leaf.

- Watch the way light plays on a surface.
- To help you, remember what it was like to be a child, when you could spend hours exploring a tiny patch of ground.

Taste sense

- Take a bite of something.
- Allow it to sit in your mouth.
- Explore it with your tongue. Notice its texture and taste.
- Notice how it feels as you swallow it.

Bodily sense

- Focus in on a neutral area.
- Go particularly for an area that isn't calling your attention, or that you'd like to relax more.
- This might be, for example, the touch of your fingers in your pocket.
- It might be the set of your jaw muscles.
- It might be the breath coming in and out of your nostrils.
- If you feel in pain, and you want to move away from a focus on that pain, focus on wherever is neutral for you.

Choose one of these senses now. Focus in on one area. Aim for ten breaths. Remember:

- Go small rather than big.
- Think of this as an experiment.
- Remove any pressure.

About the routines

In the next three sections of this chapter (*parts iv, v* and *vi*) are different everyday routines that will get you connecting to the senses:

Everyday reconnection
Before blank time
Treat yourself

During these routines, you'll choose one way to connect to the senses. It doesn't matter how you do it: with the *sense rotation, one sense focus* or *deepest focus.*

Go for what works for you, at that moment, or what you feel like doing. In general, however:

- If you're highly wired, do the *sense rotation.*
- If you're semi-frazzled, do the *one-sense focus.*
- If you're ready to go further, do the *deepest focus.*

Practice works: Mindfulness & me, part two

What they say is true: the more you reconnect with your whole self, the easier reconnecting with your whole self becomes. Choosing just one of the routines, for one minute a day, will show you that. It doesn't matter if you skip a day, or two days, or many days. The more you do, the more your brain will become used to doing it (although obviously, the more regular your habit is, the easier that will be).

This is because of neuroplasticity: the brain's ability to rewire and make new connections, to create positive, healing habits and drop ones that no longer serve us.

I can tell you this, because it's how it worked for me.

I always assumed I would never be able to connect with

mindfulness, because of the stress and pressure I was under, and because of the challenges posed by living in the middle of a busy city. Yet by removing my high-achievement tendencies, and by connecting to my whole self via the senses, using the routines on the next few pages but without the sense that I was failing, has taken me, step by step, into more of an awareness of my whole self. In fact, it has led me on a journey towards an entirely new way of framing my life.

If you discover that you're keen to reconnect further, and you have the time and funds to allow it, you'll see some tips at the end for a deeper reconnection.

However, I only ask that you give the routines a go, to discover which ones work for you, and combine them with the *sense connection exercises* above to discover your own best way into that re-engagement with your true, calmer self. If you start here, you'll find your own ways towards stilling the mind and relearning the joy of the moment.

iv) Everyday reconnection

Your daily life already contains dozens of potential ways you can connect with the senses: routines you already do. However, like any regular human being – including me – you do them with half your brain switched off.

This is for several reasons, as we'll see below.

Our switched-off brain: the supermarket example

Focus on results

We often focus on the *result* of the activity, not the *doing* of it in itself. In the supermarket, we need to buy food at the best possible price, and so we focus on getting the items on our list and searching for reductions.

Time limits

We are also time-pressured – if we only have half an hour to whiz around the shops picking things up, we won't have time to slow and still the mind.

Engagement with other people

We also are rarely on our own. We sometimes have to take small, talkative humans with us to the supermarket, which can pull us out of a whole-brain connection. In addition, the frazzled often crave distraction, and that can manifest in a constant desire to talk. The desire for company and friendship is both positive and essential, but it can also spill into areas where we might benefit from some peace and quiet. If we feel the need to make a phone call while we're in the supermarket, we'll constantly task-switch and lose focus on both the conversation and the moment of where we are, right now: nothing wins but our frazzle.

Too much exterior stimulation

We also – as I've mentioned – tend to live in busy, stimulating environments. With musak on supermarket speakers, a dizzying array of choice, avoiding both the abandoned trolley and dawdling shoppers, how are we supposed to get focused? Why wouldn't we want to switch off?

How to reconnect a switched-off brain

Despite all the above, there remains an opportunity – even for just a few seconds – to focus on a detail in what's before you, using one or more of the senses.

Once you've chosen an item, feel its texture beneath your fingers, breathe in its aroma if it has any, and focus your gaze upon it without getting dragged into analysing the ingredients list (you checked that earlier). Then put it in your trolley and move on.

That sense reconnection only took five to ten seconds out of your half-hour shop, but it was a brief respite from the hurly-burly around you, an opportunity to still your mind and reconnect, and it will help to ground and unfrazzle you.

Exercise: The sense-connection potential of your daily routines

1. In your notebook, write *any* routines that have the potential for a sense connection. If a routine doesn't seem immediately obvious, write it down anyway, and when you've made your

list, come back to it and see if you can find any way you can connect to your senses.

Tips

- Aim for activities you tend to do – or can do – alone. If you're rarely alone, think of a moment within your routine when you can take a minute for yourself. For example:

Exercise – yoga, working out, running, swimming
Hobbies – musical instruments or singing, craft activities, gardening, photography
Food-related – shopping, cooking, eating
Morning routine – brushing teeth, washing face

- Think of routines you both choose to do (like exercise) and have to do (like shopping).

2. Beside each activity, write the senses that you might be able to connect to. It's unlikely you'll be able to do a full sense rotation with each one (it's unlikely you'll be able to use taste in the supermarket, unless you feel like drawing attention to yourself), so write as many as you can think of.

3. You can also think of the sense first (eg smell) and anything you do that would enable that connection. For example:
Smell – gardening
Taste – eating
Visual – housework
Sound – cooking
Bodily sense – brushing teeth

4. Aim for five to ten different activities.

5. The next time you do one of them and you remember this list you wrote, try one of the three ways to connect to your senses (rotation, focus on one sense, focus on an area within one sense).

Quiz – What are your most and least-developed senses?

Do the quiz below to find out which sense – or senses – are more developed in you than others.
In your notebook, write the name of each sense (eg sound) and tally how many times you can answer 'Yes.'
Then count up your tally for each sense and write it alongside.

a) Sound

- Do you have a strong affinity with music?
- Can you distinguish between different types of sound (eg birdsong)?
- Are you good at imitating different accents?

b) Visual

- Do you automatically know the appropriate colour to choose (eg when decorating / buying clothes)?
- Do you find it easy to recognise different faces?

- Do shapes and patterns often call your attention?

c) Taste

- Do you make a special effort to track down unusual or special types of food?
- Have you had a career – or would you like to have one – in the food industry?
- Do you enjoy very fine, subtle tastes?

d) Bodily sense

- Do you like dancing?
- When you communicate, do you often also use gestures or another part of your body to 'speak'?
- Do you have sensitive skin?

e) Smell

- Can you often tell what perfume others are wearing?
- Do you find it easy to distinguish between different herbs and spices from scent alone?
- Do you rarely get colds / hayfever / sinus problems?

Quiz results

Look at your answers, and in your notebook write the senses in the order of points. For example:

bodily sense = 3 points
smell sense / taste sense = 2 points
visual sense = 1 point

sound sense = 0 points

In the example above, *bodily sense* is the most developed, and the *sound sense* is the least developed.

You may have become an expert in one sense because you have a natural affiliation for it. In addition, if you've developed that into a profession or consuming hobby, you'll have practised it even further. If you enjoy taste, for example, you may have then found a profession in the food industry, which would have developed your sense of taste even further.

In this case, the pathways in your brain will be better-established than other routes. It won't take so much effort for you to focus on that sense, because your brain is so well practised at it. Not only that, but people who score 3 points in several areas might be so aware of external stimulation that their brain has tipped over into hyper-sensitivity. For example, unpleasant sounds, visual images or smells might affect these people more strongly than they do other people.

Easy engagement: 2-point sense focus

As you start the routines that follow, engage with any senses for which you scored 2 points. If you don't have any, choose a 0 or 1-point scoring sense you feel will be easier to focus on.

Start, ideally, with a 2-point sense because, although it is somewhat developed in you, it's not as highly developed as a 3-point sense would be. It's a good starting point to get into the full-focus reconnection.

When you're at ease with the routines, and that full engagement with the sense feels unchallenging, go on to the challenging engagement below.

Challenge engagement: 1-point sense focus

... Or a 0-point sense focus for an even more challenging engagement. This will really help to give a workout to an under-used part of your brain, and enable a route to deeper mindfulness and a stronger connection than going to your most developed senses.

When you attempt your everyday reconnection, and during the exercises that follow this one, focus on that sense.

In the example above, the visual sense scores 1 point, so you would connect with the visual details of what's before you during the routines, without judgement or comment: the colours, shapes, patterns of nature, clothing, building detail, marks in the ground, and so on.

> **Chloe lives in Manchester. She unfrazzles by doing yoga, pilates and going on silent retreats.**
> I have a highly developed sense of where my body is in space, but I am not anywhere near as sensitive to sounds around me. It's why recently I've started taking a mindful walk home being aware of every sound, and it's been a wonderful experience.
> As I walk I notice the sound of my breath, the blood pumping through my body, the sound of my feet, the noise of other people, the air rushing past. I really pay attention to it all, and it's a really lovely experience, quite profound. Afterwards I feel like I've walked in a different world.

v) Reconnect + Blank time = Unfrazzle

As we explored together in Chapter Four, blank time is crucial for giving our brain space to breathe and unwind from stress. Yet a focused connection to our senses, or any sort of mindfulness, is antithetical to blank time.

It's because utilising the mind-wandering network of the brain – as we do in blank time – is basically allowing our monkey mind space to hop about and jump from thought to thought, which can spike us with stress.

However, this is because we don't have *enough* blank time in our day, not too much. Unless we deliberately input blank time on a regular, daily basis, stress symptoms will strike us whenever a spare moment crosses our path.

At the same time, blank time will only take us so far in unfrazzling. It's why, in the following exercises, you're going to combine at least one of your daily blank time routines with a focused reconnection to the senses. Doing them both together will enable your brain's neurons to do what's known as *fire and wire*. This basically means that when you regularly combine two activities, behaviours or thoughts – or a mixture – your brain's more likely to embed that as a habit or routine.

How to link *Reconnection* with *Blank time*

Mindful connection – even using the method I outline in this chapter – is a particular challenge for someone who has a tendency to multi-task and a habit of using the clever brain as a default. Mindfulness guides tend to be written by experts in the field. Yet the very problem with a book is that it is just that: a book. It's not a living, breathing teacher to help you

DEEPER UNFRAZZLE: HOW TO RECONNECT

reconnect to your physical self. Books need to be interpreted by the 'clever' brain – and it's the clever brain we must put aside in order to reconnect.

When I started reconnecting to my senses, I set the bar extremely low. Sometimes I only managed a few seconds. Other days, not even that. I took inspiration from others – such as my friend Mark – who have only found the process to work by releasing the pressure, not adding to it.

Over time, I've found my practice building. Week by week, it became easier to focus. That's not to say I'm an expert – far from it. But if I – with my scattered, fractured mind – can learn to fully focus, then anyone can.

When I started reconnecting to the senses, it was logical to link it to the routines in which I was in blank time: because it's where I didn't need to add anything on as an 'extra' to my day. I began with my blank time commute: before I 'rewarded' myself with blank time, I put on my headphones, plugged in my MP3 player and switched on white noise to block out the sound of chatter (after teaching a class all day, the brain automatically starts to interpret any voices around as demands for attention).

I started by actively engaging with my bodily sense, as it was the only one I could reasonably accommodate in a crowded railway carriage. Afterwards, I closed my eyes and allowed my brain to drift through blank time as the train took me back home.

Later, I began incorporating the sense connection into the *mindful walk* and the *sense-based everyday chore*. As time went on, I experimented with what worked for me, perhaps taking a mindful walk one day, engaging with the senses during a chore on the next. I found that keeping flexible helped to release any pressure around subjective notions of 'success' or 'failure'.

More recently, I've begun experimenting with visualisations as a way to get into the sense I want to connect with in – for example – that crowded railway carriage. In these, I recreate a past moment – or imagine a future one – and fully engage with the senses I imagine during the visualisation. I find they really help with enabling a sustained focus.

This might work for you once you have an established routine, and if you're at ease with the concept of visualisations. However, I suggest starting with the routines as detailed below, and only expanding once you've got into the habit.

The basics

- The next time you do your blank time activity – whether that's *public transport, the calmest walk* or *everyday tasks,* connect with the senses first.
- Do it *before* you engage with blank time. Any sort of mindfulness exercise can be a challenge, especially at the beginning, so do this first, keeping your blank time afterwards as a reward.
- You can simply try one of the *Three ways to connect* exercises (sense rotation, focus on one sense, or focus on an area within a sense).
- However, if you also want to expand to a particular guided exercise, choose one of the activities below.

Tips for reconnection before blank time

- Keep the bar low. Ten seconds is an excellent start.
- Keep flexible. Try different activities on different days.
- Adapt. Change any of the exercises to see how it works for you.
- Remember that *fire & wire* works. If you want to embed

this as a routine, adapt it into an already-existing every-day routine. This is why here, it's linked to blank time, which in turn links to an already-existing routine. You can link it to another routine as well (see *Everyday Treats* for further ideas, after this section).

- Take the pressure off. Slipping in and out of a reconnection exercise is normal. The mind regularly jumps away, reconnects, jumps away, reconnects. That, in itself, is enough for a deeper Unfrazzle.

Exercises to do anywhere (and definitely on public transport)

On public transport it can be a challenge to engage with any sense other than the bodily one. If you choose to engage with reconnection while on public transport – or being driven in a car – do one of the following exercises. However, the two exercises below can be done wherever you are – on public transport, on your calmest walk, or during an everyday chore.

Get with the breath

This involves an awareness of the bodily sense, plus possibly the auditory sense too (if you're able to hear your breath).
- Take your mind down to your belly, just below your ribs.
- Breathe in through your nose for five conscious, slow counts, allowing air to fill the bottom area of your lungs.
  - ✦ Note how the breath feels as it travels down your nostrils, through your chest, and into your belly.
  - ✦ Listen (if you can) to the sound your breath makes as it enters your body.
- After five counts, allow the breath to leave your belly for

eight slow counts. As you breathe out, relax any tension in your belly, chest, and jaw. Consciously relax each part of your body one by one.

- Repeat.

This activity can be done any time, any place, anywhere. You can link it to your pre-sleep Unfrazzle routine: do the Wind-Down Zone, then once in bed take five conscious breaths to completely let go of the day before you drift off to sleep.

One of the reasons getting with the breath is so excellent for Unfrazzle is because of our two nervous systems: the *sympathetic*: the fight-or-flight, heart-racing, stress response, and the *parasympathetic*: the relaxed, sleepy, slow heart-rate response.

Anyone who's frazzled will be operating on sympathetic. Getting with the breath automatically switches us to the relaxed, parasympathetic system.

Posture + breath

This again focuses on the bodily sense, and so can be done anywhere.

- Start with one area of your body to adjust and bring a focus to, for example by bringing yourself out of any usual slumped position, perhaps by drawing in your core.
- Then move your focus to another area. Ensure your legs and feet are in alignment, then your lower back, upper back, shoulders, neck, head, arms, hands, fingers.
- Now allow the tension to leave your body: it's often held in the back or shoulders, but can be anywhere.
- Switch focus to a breath in and out, as in the exercise above.

Take the senses for a walk

At some point during your blank time *calmest walk,* try to remember the following exercise. It involves a focus on one particular sense, but you can do it as a sense rotation instead. Walking can involve the bodily sense, auditory, olfactory (smell) and visual senses.

First, engage with your most developed senses (the one you discovered in the previous quiz). As you become more used to that, branch out to your least developed senses.

Bodily sense walk

This is a good basic exercise for anyone who can walk without an aid (if you need an aid, try one of the other sense walks). We can often be fairly engaged with aspects of our bodily sense, but the feet are often under-noticed. Focusing on the feet will help with your balance and stability.

- Put your mind into the soles of your feet.
- Set your foot on the ground, heel to toe. Take a step.
- Take another step. Notice the sensations underfoot.
- Continue for as long as you feel is appropriate, then re-engage with your blank time walk.

Visual sense walk

This is both the easiest and trickiest of the senses to engage with. Our visual sense is highly practised, but we almost always engage our clever brain alongside it. We no longer just look: we label, judge, interpret, decode.

- As you walk, let your gaze linger on visual details in turn.
- Engage with the smallest detail you can see: a blade of

grass, a sweet wrapper on the ground, the glint of sunshine on a street sign.

- However, at the same time try not to label those details as such.
- Any written information will send a message to your clever brain to decode. Let your gaze drift over any writing.
- Additionally, the brain decodes facial expressions or body language. Let your gaze drift over other people you see.
- Only linger on each detail as you pass. Then move on to the next.
- Avoid any judgement of those details (such as, *sweet wrapper = rubbish = bad, grass = nature = good*).

Auditory walk

- As you walk, focus your mind on each sound as it comes to your ears.
- Don't linger too long on any one sound: move to the next.
- Don't place judgement on any particular sound: no sound is more or less valid than the rest.
- Your mind will want to label sounds: birdsong, traffic, breeze through leaves. If you can, let all labels go. Sound is just sound.
- Then re-engage with your blank time walk.

Olfactory sense walk

- Put your mind into the sense of smell.
- Notice the quality and difference of the smells as you walk: fresh, dark, sweet, bitter.

- Your mind will want to attach labels to smells: perfume, flowers, cut grass. Let these go.
- We all have smells we prefer to others. Let go of judgement, whether good or bad.
- Smells come, go, pass. Even one fragrance changes hour to hour.

A note on the senses walk

If you're feeling overburdened with a particular area of stimuli (sound, smells, or any others), then focus on another area. Use your own judgement when deciding which of the senses walks you want to do that day. Engage with one where the stimuli available will not overburden you.

Everyday tasks to engage the senses

Look again at the list you wrote in Chapter Four on *Everyday tasks to unfrazzle*. During any of these, you can choose to spend anywhere from a few seconds upwards to really connect with one or more of the senses. Below is an example.

Cook with the senses

Cooking is an enjoyable way to engage with sense rotation, as each sense connects with the act of preparing food, and is (usually) pleasurable.

In this exercise, engage every one of the five senses in turn. You can do this as you prepare the food, as you cook it, or both. You can dip in and out of a sense focus. If you prefer, focus on just one of the senses below instead.

Visual sense

Focus on the colours and shapes of the ingredients as you prepare them: the redness of a pepper, the shape rice makes as you shake it into a pan.

Bodily sense

How does each item feel in your hands as you hold it? Feel the sense of it: the papery skin of a garlic bulb, the taut surface of a tomato. Notice the feel of the cooking implement you're using: the rubber seal of the knife handle, the rough wood of the stirring spoon.

Olfactory sense

Notice how each item smells as it releases its scent to the air: the grassy scent of oregano, the smoke of dried paprika.

Auditory sense

Switch focus to immediate sounds: the crunch of a knife blade through onion, the sizzle of oil heating in the pan.

Taste sense

As you taste the meal before serving – or at the start of your meal – take a moment to savour the mouthful, absorbing the flavours in your mouth before swallowing.

Although I have described the way the senses might come to you above, try to avoid any such labelling as you do the exercise.

It is easier when cooking to avoid judgement of the things you sense. At the same time, try not to get lost down the rabbit hole of ingredient labels and who last cleaned out the vegetable drawer. If you do, return to the senses and focus on the moment of now.

Other everyday tasks to engage the senses

Gardening

Utilise the visual, bodily, auditory and olfactory senses as you work in the garden.

Focus on how the earth feels under your hands, the colour of petals, plants or leaves, the sounds you can hear – trowel into mud, the buzz of a bee – and smells: damp earth, pungent flowers.

Putting away the washing

As you remove each item from the line, focus briefly on how it feels in your hands, the smell of clean linen, and the colour and shape it makes (without judgement over greyness or faded pinks).

Washing up

Feel the dish in your hands, smell the scent of the liquid in the water, listen to the sound of rinsing water as it sluices away the soap, notice the shape of the clean dish on the draining board.

In your notebook, write down any everyday tasks that appeal to you, where you think you might be able to engage the senses.

vi) Treat yourself

We live in a world that often places a greater value on things that can be bought and sold, rather than things we can get for free. This includes the concept of 'treats'.

A treat is often valued if it's either bought as a commercially available item, or as a service provided by others. And there are some treats that have to be bought or provided by others; but that doesn't have to be the case.

Unfrazzle is about turning the everyday into an opportunity. I've discussed how we can reframe our daily grind and our unlovely routines for Unfrazzle. But we can do so much more as well. The everyday contains opportunities for us to treat ourselves, via an engagement with the senses.

A treat is an activity that we savour and truly enjoy, however minor the treat may be, such as eating one square of chocolate. Cramming down half a bar – even if it's handmade and artisan with raw cacao – while hovering over your keyboard isn't (I speak from experience).

Below is an example exercise to use a regular life occurrence as a treat for the senses. Then you'll discover what your regular sense treats are, and I'll tell you about mine.

Wash your hair

This everyday treat utilises the bodily sense in the same way that getting a massage does. However, you can choose to focus instead, or in addition, on the olfactory sense (focusing on the scent of shampoo and conditioner) and the auditory sense (the sound of water cascading from the shower).

You can also lead in with the *get with the breath* exercise to

bring you into the same relaxed state that a masseur will do –
obviously, don't breathe in any water as you do so.

- Feel the water tumbling on your head as you rinse your hair.
- Rub the shampoo in and use the opportunity to massage
  your scalp. Focus on each area in turn: the nape of the
  neck and back of the head at the brainstem, the side of
  the head behind the ears, up to the top and over to the
  front at the hairline. Notice how your scalp feels as your
  fingers bring blood flow to the surface, and the sensation
  of shampoo and hair beneath your fingertips.
- Rinse off, again noting the sensation of water sluicing
  through your hair.
- Repeat with conditioner, if you like.

What are your treats for the senses?

In your notebook, write down the title *My treats for the senses.*

Take a moment to think about where and when you can
indulge in a full engagement with one or more of the senses
using an everyday activity *that you can provide yourself.*

Below are two examples.

Visual / auditory / bodily

*Opening the window as soon as I get up, leaning out, breathing
in the fresh morning air and looking up at the early sky. Feeling the
cold or the sun on my face.*

Taste / olfactory

*In the afternoon, sitting at my desk, taking a square of chocolate,
closing my eyes and smelling it briefly before putting it into my
mouth, rolling it around my tongue before swallowing it down.*

Do the same thing yourself. Write as many things as come into your mind, as a mind map or as a list. If you already have an everyday treat such as the ones above, the next time you do them, engage fully with the appropriate senses – without labelling, without judgement, and without pressure.

Example: My sense treat

I make a black coffee for myself in the morning and take it to the station in a flask. Sitting on the train, on the way to work before I engage with blank time, I drink my coffee, allowing the flavours and smell to penetrate my senses. Properly smelling and tasting the coffee gives me so much more enjoyment than gulping it down for the caffeine alone, and the taste lingers as I then put it away and gaze out of the window, allowing my thoughts to drift.

vii) Further senses connection: tips and ideas

If you want to engage further with the senses – with something you already do, or in a new way – below are some tips to do so. Most require extra time and funds, but if you have the opportunity, you can find within each activity ways to more deeply unfrazzle.

Try physical exercise

Whenever we exercise, we often have a choice to either properly engage the bodily sense, or to disengage and allow ourselves to drift off. It's possible that one of the appeals of a power yoga or HIIT class is that there is very little opportunity for the mind to wander. It must stay focused on the task in hand: although that doesn't always mean a true engagement with the bodily sense. It can mean that participants focus only on the activity, not the way the body engages with the activity.

Running
Connect briefly to each *smell* and *sound* as you run.

Bodily sense: focus on the ground beneath your feet, the alignment of your body, the sense of your body moving through air. It will help you to keep a good sense of balance and prevent injury.

Swimming
As with running, you can move between blank time and sense engagement as you swim (see novelist Laura Wilkinson's testimony on blank time to unfrazzle in Chapter Four). Engaging fully with the senses, especially the *bodily sense,* will

allow a deeper Unfrazzle. As you swim, focus on your legs and arms moving through the water, your core muscles, the *smell* and *sound* of the water as you move through it, and the feel of it rushing past.

Yoga

The aim of yoga is to get the mind into the body, but that doesn't mean it always happens. Attempt to focus on the moment of each pose as you're inside it, allowing the mind to enter each part of the body, ensuring alignment and preventing possible injury.

Yin yoga is excellent for a sense-based relaxation, as during this class, you hold postures for anywhere up to five minutes. Each posture is usually ground-based, either sitting or lying, and holding the pose for so long allows the body to truly relax.

Other physical exercise

The three examples above are just a few. There are so many more: gym workouts, spin classes, dance, pilates – whether taught or alone, each one offers an opportunity to really engage with the bodily sense, and is a useful way in to mindfulness, especially if you have a teacher who can get your prefrontal cortex to stop doing the work.

Have a massage

Have you ever had a 45-minute massage where you've drifted off into blank time and allowed your mind to wander from thought to thought? It can be blissful, but the benefits will be so much greater if you're able to properly engage with the bodily sense as each area is tended to.

Mindful focus on particular areas in the body as the therapist works on them will enable a deeper relaxation – and therefore Unfrazzle.

During any massage, focus your mind on the areas that therapist is working on, sensing your muscles relaxing. Particular types of massage can help with different brain areas, so experiment and see what works for you. Below are two examples.

Aromatherapy

The masseur will use scented oils on your body, each of which has a particular purpose. Focus on the smell of each one as you lie on the table, allowing it to wash through you.

Craniosacral therapy

A form of light-touch massage, done fully-clothed, that works to restore balance to the body, especially after accident or trauma. It can help to reconnect the brain to the bodily sense in a fundamental way by reducing stress and fear.

Sit in a café

People – including me – often use cafés to work, read, or catch up with friends. They're a great opportunity to get out of the house or have a break from the office, and, even without bringing anything to occupy the mind, cafés provide a chance to observe the buzz of life around and sit with one's own thoughts for a while.

However, cafés are also an opportunity to engage the senses:

Smell and *taste* to the fullest extent the drink you've bought.

Observe small details without judgement or labelling – so rather than watching people, focus on the detail of the table or the pattern of the cup.

Engage the *bodily sense* via the feeling of the cup in your hands and your body on the seat.

Although a coffee or tea in a café might only be a rare treat, it can bring a variety of benefits.

If cafés aren't your thing, try a quiet pub in the evening for the same effect.

Mindful creativity

Do you have a creative mind? Then, if you have the time and are willing to explore further, mindful creativity will get you into a deeper Unfrazzle space.

Creative mindfulness expert, writer and teacher **Wendy-Ann Greenhalgh** discusses her technique for enabling the senses to engage with our creative potential:

*"**Stop Look Breathe Create™** is a simple creative mindfulness practice that I use to keep me connected to the rich waters of life and creativity.*

STOP: press the pause button on life, slow down and find some stillness.

LOOK: see what's around you. Listen, smell, taste and touch too.

BREATHE: connect with the breath as it moves in and out of your body.

CREATE: after some time connecting with yourself and the world around you, express your experience with a doodle, a drawing, a photograph, some creative writing or any creative expression that calls to you."

Chapter Five summed up

Two ways to frazzle and unfrazzle a brain

1. Overworking the clever brain uses up brain fuel
   Unfrazzle: Connect to all brain areas equally

2. Multi-tasking uses up brain fuel and releases stress
   Unfrazzle: Focus the brain on one task or stimuli at a time, without interpretation or judgement.

Mindfulness, the Unfrazzle way
- Regular mindful awareness reduces depression and stress and can be essential for a deeper Unfrazzle.
- At the same time, it requires time and effort to still the 'monkey mind'.
- The *Unfrazzle* method works whatever your frazzle status, and however challenging your environment may be.

The most beneficial ways to engage the senses
- During an everyday routine.
- During or before your blank time.
- While giving yourself an everyday treat.

Tips for connecting to the senses
- Choose the way that is right for you, at this moment today.
- It's normal to drift in and out of engaging the senses.
- Experiment with both your most and least developed senses.
- Remove any pressure to get it 'right'.
- Aim low to start.

In a nutshell:

A zero-pressure, full engagement with one or more senses on a regular basis will get you into deeper Unfrazzle

CHAPTER SIX

UNFRAZZLE FOREVER: HOW TO STAY CALM FOR THE REST OF YOUR LIFE

Mini-Quiz: Routines & you

Think about the last time you started, or adapted, a routine that stuck for at least three months.

- What was the routine?
- How long did you do it for?
- What made the routine stick? Think about:
  - ✦ its frequency
  - ✦ a non-negotiable obligation (ie work / childcare)
  - ✦ an external influence (ie a course / financial commitment / a friend)
  - ✦ an association you had with the routine, emotional or otherwise
  - ✦ any immediately noticeable benefits

Now think about the last time you started, or adapted, a routine that didn't stick for longer than a few weeks.

- What was the routine?
- How long did you do it for?
- What made it unstick? Did any of the factors above, or lack of them, make a difference?

This book is based on swapping frazzling habits and routines for ones of Unfrazzle. But how do routines become second nature? How do we get them to stick? What makes a routine unstick?

There are a few basic tips for getting any positive change into your life on a regular basis. They are:

- do it regularly, at a rate you can reasonably manage long-term.
- commit for a set amount of time (three months might be reasonable).
- do it in tandem with a friend who takes up their own routine, even if it's unrelated to yours, and be each other's external influence: check in with, and encourage one another.
- associate the routine with something pleasurable: a blank time walk through your local green space, a Wind-Down Zone pottering around the kitchen, a moment of peace as you connect to the senses... whatever works for you.
- celebrate any benefits you notice, however small. If not using your phone so much means you got more work done that day, cheer yourself on.

However, this plan is also more than just routines. For me, it's become a way of life. It's now my go-to method for recovering calm whenever things get too much. Each time, I don't need to reinvent the wheel and attempt to fathom how to get my brain back, because I have the answer right here.

In fact, this book is a manifesto as much as a guide. And if you're also interested in how to incorporate everything you've read as a way of being, so you move through life with calm and ease, then this final chapter is for you. On the following pages you'll find **four ways to unfrazzle forever:**

Keep flexible
Be aware
Take permission
Return to the book

As you read this chapter, you'll discover exactly **how** and **why** these four ways are crucial to a life of Unfrazzle. You'll also get a brief summary of each chapter of the book, and a few exercises and tips to keep yourself in the zone of Unfrazzle.

Like the 'extra tips' in Chapters Three, Four and Five, some of the exercises in this chapter involve you adding an extra into your regular routine. Read the chapter through, and decide whether you have the time and space now to do so. If not, there'll be a moment in the future, and keep that in mind as you work through this last part of the book.

i) Keep flexible

We are born with billions of neurons, pulsing with potential synaptic connections. From then on, those neurons start to die.

Even as we reach out to the world, as our neurons attempt to make those connections, absorbing the lessons of life, they begin disappearing. And there is nothing we can do about it.

Year upon year, neurons vanish. By the time we're adults, we've lost around half a billion, and so they continue dying, and are – mostly – irreplacable.[7]

However, those gone-forever neurons are not necessarily the reason that as humans become older, they often become more inflexible of mind and body. In fact, all you can say about a neuron is that it has *potential*. It has the potential to spark connections, and it has the potential not to do so. A younger person has the ability to learn a second language more fluently and faster than an older person – but if they don't learn the language, that potential remains unused.

Anyone who can keep their brain flexible throughout their life will keep their neurons more active, and will be more adaptable to change. An adaptable brain will be better able to pick up and stick to a new routine. It will be better able to switch its focus from frazzle to Unfrazzle. The more positive connections that fizz from your remaining neurons, the more alive and vibrant your brain will be, and the healthier you'll be, as a result.

I learned this the hard way. I used to think I had a flexible, adaptable brain – in fact I was stuck in a total rut, but because I was forty and everybody else my age appeared to be like

---

7   At the time of writing, a neuroscientific debate is raging over this, but the consensus is that, in general, any new neurons grown by the brain are minimal.

me, I didn't even notice. It seemed obvious that I couldn't be as sharp, as flexible, as easygoing as I was when I was twenty one – that, I thought, was just what happened as you aged.

When the rug was pulled from under my feet, my brain just couldn't cope. It was already in a rut of searching for frazzle and wired for stress, and I hadn't learned anything new in the longest time. It was a harsh shock, and the consequences shone a spotlight on the realities of how I'd been before.

On the other hand, although I wouldn't recommend a crisis for shaking you out of your routine, that's what happened to me. My neurons were catapulted into action, and as a result I found myself becoming a much more flexible person.

I'm not the only one: it's why people can take up marathon-running after a divorce, or start a new career after the death of a parent. Accountants become artists. Drifters become focused. Change – even unwanted change – means we discover a more flexible brain, able to see new branches in life's path.

A flexible brain is one that is more adaptable. If you feel it impossible to change your routines so they look after you: if you pick up your phone even after reading Chapter Two, or are still not giving yourself blank time in your day after reading Chapter Four, then remember that you *can* and *will* change things, if you start exercising your brain.

At the same time, the brain is wired to want to slip into old patterns, especially those deep-wired ones of stress and frazzle. That's why, if you want to feel more adaptable to a life of reclaimed calm, there are two ways to keep a flexible brain:

1. Do exercise
2. Learn new things

Both these require you to carve some time out of your already-packed schedule (unless you already do exercise or are learning new things, of course). But if you can swap one routine for another, or demand some time for yourself (see *part iii* for tips on how to do this), you'll have habits in place that can last, in one form or another, for the rest of your life.

1. Do exercise

If you already have a regular exercise regime, you'll know its benefits. But now you also know that as well as keeping you calmer and less frazzled immediately, in the longer term it also keeps your brain flexible.

Exercise is good for the brain in many ways, too many to list here. Different types of exercise will have different effects. In addition, because we're all different, there'll be a particular combination of exercises that work for you.

If you already do regular exercise:

Try a new type of exercise (this works in tandem with the second part of keeping flexible, *learn new things*). Keep experimenting, and monitor how you feel afterwards. Gyms and yoga studios are good for this, as they often have different classes within the same building, making it easier for you to try something new. I've recently been going to Pilates, and I can almost feel my brain squeaking as it works out how to exercise rarely-used muscle groups.

If you don't already do regular exercise:

Don't leap in at the deep end (metaphorically or literally). We all know someone – possibly ourselves – who bought a year's gym membership, went five times a week for a fortnight, and then couldn't face going back.

Start small. Walking is excellent exercise, and also gives you blank time and the senses connection. Plus it's free, so what's not to like? You never know, it may lead to running, which may lead to your first 5k. But even if it doesn't, it's exercise all the same.

If you're not well enough to walk, then lie in bed and lift a bottle of water just once. Do that every day and see how quickly your fitness builds. Start as small as you feel able to.

2. Learn new things

Learning new things is difficult: it's supposed to be. If something comes easy, that area of our brain is already flexible. That doesn't mean we shouldn't learn 'easy' things, but to keep our brain flexible all over, it's important to learn things that don't come so easily. So what new things should you learn? Try the quiz to find out.

Quiz: What's difficult for you?

1. Do you speak more than one language well?

2. Can you sing or play a musical instrument?

3. Are you good with numbers?

4. Do you create art / write fiction or poetry?

5. Are you good with directions and map-reading?

6. Do you know a lot about plants and flowers?

7. Do you regularly cook or bake from scratch?

8. Are you good at sewing, knitting, or other crafts?

9. Can you follow written instructions easily?

10. Are you good at spelling?

Answers

Don't add up how many times you answered 'yes' or 'no.' In fact, the more times you answered 'no', the better. Because if you want to know what you should learn, look at those 'no' answers. That doesn't mean you have to learn how to sew (for example). But it will give you a clue as to what you might want to learn.

As with exercise, start small (and, of course, you can combine the two, by learning a new type of physical exercise). If you can't follow written instructions easily, start by following *one* recipe, to the letter, without deviating. On the other hand, if you don't create art or write fiction or poetry, then start by sketching your hand in your notebook now, and promise you won't show it to anyone. Every week, sketch it again. Bit by bit, you'll see how much better you'll get. You can almost feel your neurons creaking to life. Sketch your hand every week for a year, and see the difference it makes: not only to your drawing ability, but to your brain.

Detention stories – Karim

The people who survive indefinite detention in the calmest way are the ones who keep learning new things. Many of the things we offer they have never done before, such as learning craft skills or writing a poem. Learning something new opens another door in the brain, a way out of the stress loop all of them are stuck in. It can't solve their problems, but it is a tiny escape, for a while, from their very difficult position.

I've met many inspirational guys in the centre. One of them, Karim, wound up in the UK some time after swimming across the Mediterranean Sea to escape his native country (and ended up in a life-threatening coma as a result). He could neither read nor write in his own or any other language, and was in his thirties when I met him, when the brain has already lost many of the neurons it was born with. He also spoke one word of English when I met him: "Hello." Nevertheless, he came to class every day, and starting with the basics, taught himself to read and write. He ended up in the detention system for over a year, being transferred from centre to centre. Eventually, he came back to the one I work in.

I was astonished. In a little over a year, in what would be a high-stress environment for anybody, with a challenging past and an unknown future, he had not only learned to speak English, but he could read and write it as well. I have met other guys who have learned to read and write English despite being illiterate in their native language, but most of them were much younger when they started to learn. Karim's story tells me that those who keep dedicated and flexible to learning new things are the ones who survive.

Exercise: Quick memory task

One more way you can build your flexible brain is by mini-memory exercises like the one below. Anyone can do this, and it will help all of us. This sort of exercise works the hippocampus, the memory-forming area of the brain.

1. Write a shopping list.
2. Group three or more items together.
3. Try whatever works to help you remember them: chanting them aloud, picturing them written down, picturing them on the shelf.
4. Go shopping and pick up those three items.
5. Use the list to check you were right, and to buy the rest of your items.

You can adapt this for ingredients from a recipe you're about to cook, or for directions for a route you don't know. Experiment. See what makes your brain crackle to life.

ii) Be aware

Before I started the process of Unfrazzle, I had a horror at the thought of being bored. I thought spending time doing 'nothing' was wasted. I was late for everything because I couldn't bear to be early. In queues, I was impatient. I got irritated at dawdlers. I walked fast. I enjoyed the swiftness of my movements.

Perhaps it's a stretch to say I welcome boredom, but I can handle it. I'm able to gaze out of the window at nothing. I can leave on time. I embrace queues (sort of). I slow down behind slower people without grumbling *too* much. I've changed, and it was almost without realising it.

But before you think I'm too smug, I ought to let you know that the above is only true some of the time.

The other part – which occupies a higher percentage of my daily life than I like to admit – is a battle between my old, established behaviours and attitudes, and the more recent ones. As I've moved on in my journey, I can feel the old habits falling away, but I'm hardly at Buddhist-monk levels of Zen. And if I tell myself that I've got everything sorted now, I might as well be back in the old days, when, strung-out and sleepless, I felt secure in the delusion that I was just the *right side* of stress.

Awareness has two parts:
The first is celebrating how things have already changed, even in such a short space of time.
The second is acknowledging where we are in the process, and that things are changing, and will continue to do so.

Awareness is hard, because however awake and truthful I think I'm being, there's always a part of me that has its hands over my eyes and fingers in ears, chanting *la la la*.

What about you? For example, did you plump for any answers in the quizzes that were how you *wanted* to be, rather than how you are, right now?

But awareness works two ways, because if we're three hundred and sixty degrees aware, we'll also know that things have the potential to change.

I can't tell you with absolute certainty that I'm totally aware of my frazzle when it hits. How can I possibly know? When we're frazzled, we find it hard to grapple with the basics of life, never mind anything more.

However, each time I *do* notice my frazzle, I return to the Unfrazzle routines. And because I've been doing them such a long time, they are now much easier to do. In case you've forgotten, I wasn't a natural at this when I started. I was wired to the max, highly perfectionist, and constantly busy. But simply being aware of frazzle meant I started reframing my routines – and then I ended up changing my life.

Exercise: A moment for reflection & positive affirmations

These exercises work on the first part of awareness, **celebrating how things have changed**. It is also an opportunity to create *positive affirmations*, where writing something as if it is true helps to forge a route in the brain that tells us it is true.

Go back to the exercise in Chapter One, *Write a positive future*. In it, you wrote a few things you wanted for a specific future, and a few things you wanted for a wider future.

Specific future

- Look at what you wrote for your **specific future.**
- Take a moment to think about how close or far away you are from achieving that aim.
- Whether you've achieved it or not, copy the same lines into your book, but remove the line *would like to.*

For example, instead of:
I would like to get the headspace to read a book.

Write instead:
I get the headspace to read a book.

If you are closer to achieving this than before, take a moment to celebrate the work you've put in, in order to get to this goal. Actually, take more than a moment. Take all day. Treat yourself. Do something special. You're amazing.

If you are no closer to achieving this than before, take time to absorb the statement as if it were true, right now. Rewiring the brain to get into a mindset you'd like is a complex process, and accepting a statement as 'true' even though you know it's not, is one method to help reroute neurons along a different path. It's a neurological case of 'fake it till you make it.'

Wider future

- Now look at what you wrote for your **wider future**.
- Each of those grand ambitions are a process that you are already

going through. The process started when you picked up this book and began to read.

- It doesn't matter whether you have calm days or anxious days, whether you still get frazzled, whether you're just as much of a perfectionist as before.
- None of that matters, because all of that *can* and *will* improve.
- Now write all your sentences again, but change each sentence to the present tense.
- In addition, use positive language where you can, rather than negative.

For example, instead of:
I would like to be a calmer, happier person.

Write:
I am a calmer, happier person.

Instead of:
I would like to not fear being bored.

Write:
I embrace under-stimulation [as 'fear' and 'bored' have negative connotations].

These again are positive affirmations. Writing them as if they were true is one route to making sure they do come true. Return to these as often as you like. Repeat them to yourself. Each day, week, month, year, is a step forwards in the process of Unfrazzle.

Exercise: notice your frazzle

This exercise works on the second part of awareness, **acknowledging where you are in the process.** It also brings us almost full circle, back to Chapter One where you assessed your frazzle status in the quiz.

1. Return to the **Quiz: What's your frazzle status?** in Chapter One, part i). There's no need to do the quiz again, unless you want to: you'll already know it by now, I guess.

2. In your notebook, write **my symptoms of frazzle.**

3. Now write any particular symptoms of frazzle that you feel are yours. If you only want to write the two or three most important ones for you, do so. If you'd rather copy them all out, do that instead.

However, instead of the longer phrase from the quiz, you're going to turn them into general statements.
For example, instead of writing *I feel more easily irritated than I used to,* write *feeling irritated.*
Instead of *I feel there are too many problems I can't solve,* write *too many problems.*

4. Keep the list in your notebook, or tear it out and put it in your wallet, but in a secret spot that you won't look at all the time. You don't want to be told *too many problems* every day, after all, even if it's true.

5. Removing the *I feel* removes any negative sensations the list

might evoke. What you have now is a list of frazzle symptoms. Check the list whenever you think things might be getting on top of you, and if you can tick more than half of them, instantly return to the routines in the book (go to *part iv* of this chapter to find out more).

iii) Take permission

One of the hardest things I've learned about myself in this process is that fundamentally, I used to believe that I didn't deserve to unfrazzle.

The reason I mention it here is because what I've observed from the frazzled amongst us is that so many of us have this in common:

We don't believe we deserve Unfrazzle

It's not only habit that means we cling on to our stress routines, why we rush from place to place, why we feel over-whelmed and yet find it hard to make the fundamental changes required. Deep down, we think we ought to be frazzled.

It's a strange, fascinating concept, and is a topic that could be explored in much depth. It's also merely the outward thread of a tangled web involving a multitude of factors.

You may accept what I believe, or you may not. That doesn't matter, because this section of the book wants to tell you:

You deserve Unfrazzle

Exercise: Do you believe you deserve Unfrazzle? (Part One)

Note any of the following sentences that you agree with.

- Taking time out is a necessity.
- Being unavailable, every day, if only for a short time, is a necessity.

- Delegating where possible is a necessity.
- Saying no to others, and yes to myself, is a necessity.
- Doing what I need to do for Unfrazzle is a necessity.

Exercise: Do you believe you deserve Unfrazzle? (Part Two)

Look again at the sentences above. I imagine you probably agree with the majority of those statements. It should be obvious that taking time out is a necessity in order to preserve our mental wellbeing, for example.

However – and be honest – how many of those actions *do you actually do?* Do you take time out? Do you make yourself unavailable every day? Or are you thinking, *Well, of course I'd love to, but it's just not possible because of X/Y/Z…*

It's OK, I've got you. And I understand, because I've been there. During the crisis, there were times when things were really, really bad, and when I *felt* as if I had to be available every moment that I didn't have to be at work. It was a self-imposed prison, but I told myself that being unavailable meant something awful would happen, and that because I wasn't the one seriously ill then my needs were trivial in comparison.

It was a nonsense, and an unhelpful one at that, but hindsight always has 20/20 vision. I felt that the great irony of the universe would ensure that the minute I stopped being 'there', the world would fall apart.

And here's the thing: stuff happened when I was there, and when I wasn't, and I didn't make that much difference either way. I wasn't as God-like as I'd imagined.

You might think you need to be available, and you don't have a single moment for time out, but I hope that if this book has shown you anything, it's that the time is there, and you just need to give yourself permission to take it.

Learn from my experience: whether you want to or not, you both deserve and need Unfrazzle, so make sure you get the time to do so.

Exercise – further positive affirmations (non-achievement based)

In part ii), you wrote down some positive achievement-based affirmations such as *I embrace under-stimulation*.

As valuable as these are, it's important to recognise that we might be tempted to view our progress in terms of 'success' or 'failure.' A part of us always will always crave stimulation, even if it's just 10%. The dopamine neurons in our brain mean we crave excitement. It's neurological, that's all.

To counteract that, below are some non-achievement based affirmations. Choose any that appeal to you and write them in your notebook in big letters.

If you have any different ones, write those instead, or in addition.

I deserve to remain focused without stress.

I deserve to fulfil my duties and responsibilities without stress.

I deserve to reclaim my true calm.

I deserve to feel free.

I deserve a life of Unfrazzle.

iv) Return to the book

I have made a new life based around Unfrazzle. Yet as the saying goes, old habits die hard. The pattern goes something like this:

Become frazzled.

↓

Turn to Unfrazzle routines.

↓

Feel calmer, clearer, happier. Notice less anxiety, less of a reaction to stress, better sleep, better everything.

↓

Notice able to use phone with less frazzle = use phone more.

↓

Less frazzled in evening = evenings become hectic.

↓

Calmer every day = forget blank time and ignore sense connection.

↓

Become frazzled.

Etc.

Can we all be honest, and admit that we're only human? It's why I, for one, need a manual such as this. The routines exist so we can return to them, to remind ourselves of our deep need to unfrazzle and return to the calmer person we know we are inside.

In this section, you'll read a summary of all the chapters in the book. You can return to this part if you become frazzled again and want a brief reminder of which chapter to return to, specifically. It's also a reminder, right now, of the journey of the book. They are basically a nutshell version of the summaries at the end of each chapter.

This book is as prescriptive or as loose as you need it to be. Adapt all and any of the exercises and routines so they work for you, in your life right now. I can only tell you that the routines, as I've written them here, have worked 100% for me, a person wired for maximum frazzle who found a calmer path.

Quiz: Which section of the book do you need?

Perhaps you've noticed you're getting frazzled again (see the exercise on **my symptoms of frazzle** in *part ii* of this chapter). Or perhaps, now you've finished the book, you want a reminder of which exercises tackle which specific issues. If so, answer the questions in the quiz below.

If you answer *yes,* then go to that particular chapter. If you answer *yes* to more than one, go to the earliest chapter you require, and work forwards from there.

Are things so bad that this book feels like a sticking plaster on a gaping wound?
Go to Chapter 1, part iii: How to survive extreme frazzle.

Do you need an overall reminder, a general rule for how to live a life less frazzled?
Go to Chapter 1, part iv: Your frazzle values.

Do you want to check whether your phone use has crept up again?
Go to Chapter 2, part ii: Quiz – How phone addicted are you?
Then go to one of the three recommended methods for beating the emotional brain in part v.
Then go to the exercise in part vi to remind yourself of your frazzle stop.

Do you need reminding of the feel-good loop?
Return to Chapter 2, part vii: The feel-good loop.

Do you still use your phone as an alarm clock?
Go to Chapter 3, part i: Take yourself off high alert at night.

Do you need reminding of what your foundational evening routine is?
Go to Chapter 3, part iii: A foundational routine that works for you.

Have you noticed yourself unable to settle during the evening?
Return to Chapter 3, part iv: The Wind-Down Zone.

Do you need a reminder of extras to add in to your life that may help you sleep?
Return to Chapter 3, part v: Tips for sleep.

Do you need reminding of why you need blank time?
Return to Chapter 4, part iv: Mini-quiz – What do you need blank time for?

Do you want to refresh the blank time in your life?

Return to Chapter 4, part v: Your new blank time routines. Choose another of the routines, or do one you've tried before in a different situation. See what works for you.

Do you want to put a few more extras in your life to get some deeper blank time?

Return to Chapter 4, part vi: Tips for extra blank time.

Are you still struggling with mindful awareness?

Return to Chapter 5, part iii: Get into the senses.

Do you want a reminder of how to connect blank time with a senses connection for a deeper Unfrazzle?

Go to Chapter 5, part v: Reconnect + blank time = Unfrazzle.

Are you still struggling to truly enjoy your everyday treats?

Return to Chapter 5, part vi: Treat yourself.

FINAL WORD

Welcome to the end of the book. You deserve a celebration. You deserve to feel good, and joyful, for all the efforts you've put in so far to unfrazzle yourself. Making the decision to wind the clock back from learned stress habits and patterns is the first step to changing things for the better. Believe me, I know.

There'll be times when you make a huge leap forward. There'll be times when progress seems non-existent. (I've been there too). Unfrazzle isn't a linear journey; it's forwards, then a little back, then forwards again, and so on. Life has a habit of sending us bumps in the road, just as it always has. The difference now is that you have a set of tools that you can use whenever necessary. Remember this:

Unfrazzle is a journey you can travel for the rest of your life.

Good luck as you go into the future, and let's meet again on the Unfrazzle road. I look forward to seeing you there.

Acknowledgements

This book has been a huge collaborative effort, and I owe a massive debt of thanks to everyone I met to whom I talked about the project, and who championed it right from the start, all the way through to where it is now, who kept telling me: *The world needs a book like this. Write it!* If you helped me, and I have left you out of this list, I can only apologise and beg your forgiveness. I am, as I often need to remind myself, only a human.

Firstly, Kate Harrison for taking a collection of ideas in my head and getting me to understand what I wanted to write, and why. Our conversations shaped the book from the start, and made it head just where it needed to: in the right direction.

Secondly, Wendy Ann Greenhalgh, for sharing her considerable knowledge of writing, easy mindfulness, creativity and mindful social media. Thank you also for being an early champion of the project when it needed one.

Anna Hogarty, thank you for seeing what huge potential this book had right from the initial proposal, and also for your sterling work editing my first scrappy manuscript and shaping it into something much better.

Holly Dawson, a deep bow to you for giving up your time and advice: your enthusiasm for mixing memoir with practical advice was invaluable, and worked, as I hope you see.

Siobhan Curham, a huge debt of thanks – not only for your fantastic copy-edit, but all the cheering you've done for the *Unfrazzle* project and all the advice you gave as it neared its final draft.

To all the friends who have either read parts of the book, provided much-needed feedback, or given me their own particular Unfrazzles (or frazzles), I thank you: Chris, Laura, Christine, Mark, Jasmine, Chloe, Cat, Daisy, Bel and Mich. You've all been amazing. Especial thanks to Jo and Kiran for all of the above, plus nearly thirty years of friendship, plus being total inspirations. Big love.

Thanks also to Robyn Puglia for her knowledge of how people get ill, and how they recover. Most of my research into neuroscience began at your book recommendations: thank you.

Thank you also to Dot Sutcliffe for kindly proofreading my final manuscript. Any remaining errors are, of course, all mine.

Thank you to my mum Angela for the extra proofread. More than that, however, thank you to her, David and Gabby for being so supportive over the past four years, both during the crisis and as I emerged out the other side. I am so, so lucky in my brilliant family.

Thank you also to all the guys I've met in detention over the past twenty years. Thank you for inspiring and challenging me, and showing me the amazing variance of the human spirit. I wouldn't have been able to write this book without learning from you.

Finally, to my first reader and champion, my partner Sam: you have given me so much more than I can ever express in words. Thank you isn't enough, but it will have to do: thank you.

RESOURCES & REFERENCES

Neuroscience

During my exploration into neuroplasticity, the effects of stress on the brain, and how to recover the calmer self that's inside, I read a number of inspiring, informative books by neuroscientists. If you're interested in learning more of the science behind how our brain becomes frazzled, and how it can be rewired, then you might find these helpful. I particularly recommend *The Brain that Changes Itself* as an inspirational look at how even people with severe brain injuries have recovered through rewiring their neuronal connections.

The page numbers cited are where the brief quotes in *Unfrazzle* have been taken from.

The Brain that Changes Itself: Stories of Personal Triumph from the Frontiers of Brain Science, Norman Doidge, Penguin Books 2008, p106

The End of Alzheimer's: The First Programme to Prevent and Reverse the Cognitive Decline of Dementia, Dale Bredesen, Vermilion 2017, pp196-7

The Organized Mind: Thinking Straight in the Age of Information Overload, Daniel Levitin, Penguin Books 2014, pp96-97

Why Isn't My Brain Working? A Revolutionary Understanding of Brain Decline and Effective Strategies to Recover your Brain's Health, Datis Kharrazian, Elephant Press 2013, pp99-100

Why We Sleep: The New Science of Sleep and Dreams, Matthew Walker, Penguin Books 2018, p50, 52

Wellbeing

I've read, and continue to read, many books on how to access aspects of calm, inner balance, and the peace that resides inside. I'm sure you have your own list – but if you want to add any more, here are a few of my recommendations. After reading both Wendy Ann's and Siobhan's books I contacted them to ask how on earth *I* could write a wellbeing book as good. Luckily, they provided not only helpful advice, but bags of enthusiasm for the Unfrazzle project.

 Stop Look Breathe Create: Four easy steps to mindfulness through creativity, Wendy-Ann Greenhalgh, Ilex Press 2017. A practical, illustrated guide to accessing mindfulness via mini-drawing, writing or photography exercises.

Something More: A Spiritual Misfit's Search for Meaning, Siobhan Curham, Piatkus, 2019. A personal exploration into spiritual practices combined with easy exercises to get the best out of each one.

Making Friends With Anxiety: A warm, supportive little book to ease worry and panic, Sarah Rayner, new ed. 2019. During the first year of the crisis, I read the first edition of Making Friends With Anxiety. It was what I needed; a supportive friend in book form that understands the days when you want to Ctrl-Alt-Delete the day and start again.

Breathe Magazine. If Unfrazzle were a magazine, it would be Breathe. It has tons of features on practical ways to live a good life, beautifully illustrated. I write their back-page column with my own take on everyday escapes, plus regular longer pieces on creativity, fiction and wellbeing.

Say hello

Come and say hello to me online (or in person, if I'm at an event). I'm on Twitter **@StephanieLam1** and on Instagram @ **Stephanie_Lam_1.** I love to meet other Unfrazzlers – however, I try to stay mindful of how frazzling social media can be, and so I don't check in every day. If you don't hear from me immediately, have patience, and I'll be there soon.

You can also find me on my website **stephanielam.co.uk** – where you can find out about my other writing, if you're interested.

And if you've enjoyed this book, or if you think someone else might benefit from a bit of unfrazzling – then please do spread the word! I don't have a marketing team behind me or a big publisher pushing my stuff. I'm relying instead on YOU – proper people power – to get the book out into the world.

You can also rate the book on Amazon (even if you haven't bought it there, good reviews boost the book in the algorithms). In return you'll get a huge dose of Unfrazzle love from me.